THE PUPPY HEAD START

A Complete Guide to Selecting, Raising, and Training the Puppy of Your Dreams!

THE PUPPY HEAD START

A Complete Guide to Selecting, Raising, and Training the Puppy of Your Dreams!

AMY PISHNER

A POST HILL PRESS BOOK
ISBN: 979-8-89565-257-2
ISBN (eBook): 979-8-89565-258-9

The Puppy Head Start:
A Complete Guide to Selecting, Raising, and Training the Puppy of Your Dreams!

Cover design by Jim Villaflores

This book, as well as any other Post Hill Press publications, may be purchased in bulk quantities at a special discounted rate. Contact orders@posthillpress.com for more information.

Although every effort has been made to ensure that the personal and professional advice present within this book is useful and appropriate, the author and publisher do not assume and hereby disclaim any liability to any person, business, or organization choosing to employ the guidance offered in this book.

Post Hill Press
New York • Nashville
posthillpress.com

Published in the United States of America
1 2 3 4 5 6 7 8 9 10

IN LOVING MEMORY—
This book is dedicated to Havok,
the best puppy there ever was.

TABLE OF CONTENTS

INTRODUCTION

Welcome! This book is designed to give you all the information you need to successfully raise and train your puppy.

Raising a puppy is work; let's work smarter, not harder! With the right information at your fingertips and the right tools in your toolbox, you can breeze through the training process and *enjoy* your new puppy every step of the way.

The information you will find in this book is the result of more than a decade of experience training thousands of dogs of all ages, needs, and temperaments, whether they were family, police, service, or personal protection dogs.

Puppy training is one of my favorite aspects of dog training. It is so rewarding! With the correct foundation, a puppy is ready to take on the world!

In these pages, I use my experience to give you a proven roadmap to success. I teach *what* to do, *why* to do it, *when* to do it, and *how* to do it. I also help you avoid common pitfalls in puppy training. These topics include puppy selection, preparing for your puppy, owner education, the first forty-eight hours, potty training, crate training, biting and jumping, obedience training, socialization and exposure, puppy play, health and wellness, problem-solving, and more!

This Puppy Head Start book is comprised of modified written content from my online puppy training course called The Puppy Head Start program. You can find The Puppy Head Start course and other dog training courses on my virtual training platform: Valor K9 Academy Online® by visiting our website at www.valork9academyonline.com or by scanning the QR code below with your smart phone camera:

I have designed this book and program to be the most comprehensive on-demand puppy training content in the world. It is specifically designed for puppies eight to twenty-four weeks of age but can be used on dogs of all ages who can benefit from a strong training foundation, confidence building, and proper socialization and exposure.

Puppy training is simple, but it is not easy because there is so much conflicting information online. Allow me to use my experience to streamline and simplify *everything* for YOU.

I leave no stone unturned and no question unanswered.

Before we jump in, let me formally introduce myself.

ABOUT ME

My name is Amy Pishner. I am the founder, owner, and head trainer of Valor K9 Academy and Valor Protection Dogs®. I am a triple-certified dog trainer, and I have worked with thousands of dogs in various settings.

My love for dogs began when I was a little girl. Born in Wyoming and raised in Wisconsin, I spent most of my time with my best friend, a rescued collie named Lady. We did everything together! Show-and-tells, tricks, contests, agility training at the local park, and sled dogging through quiet streets on cold winter days.

Lady is the reason I fell in love with dogs. Her love and loyalty were endless.

Lady at my childhood home in Neenah, Wisconsin, circa 1994.

A self-starter with a love for learning, I was homeschooled and then graduated public high school at the age of sixteen. After high school, I went to Ghana, West Africa, for six months on a mission trip before heading off to college. I graduated *magna cum laude* from Carthage College in Wisconsin with degrees in international political economy and Spanish. Upon graduating, I went to Ecuador, South America, for eight months to teach English and economics. When I returned stateside, I joined the Air Force and worked in military intelligence. I was stationed in North Carolina and spent most of my free time volunteering by teaching English to Mexican immigrants and by being an interpreter for a human trafficking nonprofit. Any other spare time was spent volunteering at the local animal shelter.

Training dogs and teaching people quickly became my two biggest passions. At the shelter, I was especially drawn to puppies and soon became a foster parent for them. The shelter allowed me to take young puppies home with me to start their training and find homes for them. Over a six-month period, I fostered and rehomed thirty-six puppies. To further my education and personal cause, I started fostering, training, and rehoming adult dogs with various kinds of behavioral issues.

I met Justin, my husband, friend, and business partner, at Seymour Johnson Air Force Base in Goldsboro, North Carolina. It was then that I adopted my first dog, Zoey, a five-month-old Australian shepherd who came from a backyard breeder who abused and neglected her. The breeder's kids pulled her hair and poked her in the eyes. She lived in the mud under his back porch. She was very skittish and fearful.

Despite all that, I knew from the moment I saw her that she was meant to be mine. There was something about her that reminded me so strongly of my childhood border collie. They had the same eyes, the same mannerisms, and the same past.

It was love at first sight, but did she give me a run for my money! I had never worked with such a fearful dog before.

Zoey's behavioral issues presented an enormous challenge, but after a year of love, dedication, and endless work to overcome her fears, it was like I had found the pot of gold at the end of the rainbow. It was a magical connection.

Week after week, she became a different dog, a better version of herself. Close to the one-year anniversary of her Gotcha Day (the day I adopted her), she passed the stringent requirements to become a certified therapy dog at a local mental health facility. She wowed the patients with her tricks and training. It made my heart so happy to see how far she had come.

Zoey is the reason I fell in love with dog training.

Amy and Zoey, circa 2013.

Shortly after I adopted Zoey, I adopted a dog who I named Duke. Duke was a goofy German shepherd who lacked obedience and manners. After I trained Duke to be the dog he was always meant to be, I was officially hooked on training dogs. I started helping friends and coworkers with theirs and seeing the same results in them as I had in my dogs.

When I got out of the military, I pursued my passion for training and went through dog trainer schools. First, I attended Starmark Academy in Texas, where I learned the basics in obedience, behavior rehabilitation, and dog sports. From there, I went to Vohne Liche Kennels in Indiana and worked with single and dual-purpose military and police K9s. I later studied at The Michael Ellis School for Dog Trainers. With all this under my belt, I knew it was time for me to start my own method of dog training and that is when it was born: The VK9 Method™.

Amy and police K9 Lady, circa 2013.

I started working with clients in 2013. In April of 2014, I moved to Chattanooga, Tennessee, and officially opened Valor K9 Academy. In June of 2015, I moved to Spokane, Washington, and, with my husband, Justin, we opened a second location. In June of 2019, we moved to Boise, Idaho, where we are now located and have opened a third location.

At our largest, we had all three locations in operation with fifteen trainers and team members, all hand-picked and trained by me. For many years, I worked eighty to ninety hours a week and personally trained around five hundred dogs each month via private lessons, group classes, workshops, seminars, and board and trains.

In June of 2021, Justin and I opened Valor Protection Dogs, my dream business, where we import, raise, and train elite German shepherds for service work and personal protection.

Valor Protection Dogs Zion, Havok, Duke, and Freya, circa 2022.

They say, "Do what you love and love what you do," and that most certainly rings true for me!

MY PHILOSOPHY

What is my puppy training philosophy?

Do you remember the story of "The Three Little Pigs"?

Fatty and Hammy quickly built their houses out of straw and sticks. When the wolf appeared, he huffed, and he puffed, and he blew their houses down.

On the other hand, Porky the pig built his house out of bricks. Even though it took him longer to do it, his house was strong, it did not blow down, and it kept the three little pigs safe from the wolf.

My training philosophy is much like Porky's. I believe that if you are going to do something, do it right. This is why my training focuses on building a strong foundation first.

For puppies, this foundation training includes: communication, motivation, and relationship; socialization and exposure; confidence building; and obedience training and manners.

I use primarily positive reinforcement—like food and praise—to teach puppies what I want them to do while incorporating a slip lead (leash) to shape behavior and stop unwanted behavior. To achieve the results that every dog owner dreams about, my training focuses on clear communication, high motivation, and a healthy owner-dog relationship. I prioritize setting puppies up for success by providing structure and meeting their needs for physical exercise, mental stimulation, and training.

A tired dog is a good dog!

I also pay close attention to the dog's physical health and wellness. To truly train a dog, you must focus on the whole dog, not just certain aspects. Diet affects behavior, and behavior affects everything!

Puppies trained using my methods are happy, confident, and obedient. They are active learners who are engaged in the training process and love to learn. My end goal is to set puppies up for success. I strive to help puppies become go-anywhere, do-anything dogs who are comfortable in their own skin, well-behaved, and are enjoyable for other people to be around.

I want to help dog owners like YOU feel calm, confident, and in control. I want you to be a great pack leader for your puppy!

1.

PUPPY SELECTION

"Puppy selection is the most important first step in raising the dog of your dreams."

–Amy Pishner

In this chapter, I take you through the process of selecting a puppy. My goal is to pave the way for you to pick the right puppy for your home and family. From lifestyle and breeds to sourcing and temperament testing, I help you every step of the way!

If you already have a puppy, I still encourage you to read this chapter when you have time. It is going to help you better understand your puppy, which will benefit you as you raise and train them.

This is an information-packed chapter because getting the right puppy is the best first step for a lifetime of happiness and compatibility with your new companion.

Let's begin!

PUPPY SELECTION: A THREE-STEP PROCESS

Picking out a puppy is more than going online and looking for puppy advertisements. You need to do your homework first so that you are looking in the right direction to begin with.

When it comes to selecting a puppy, there are three important steps:

1. Selecting a breed
2. Choosing a breeder (or rescue)
3. Picking a puppy

I am going to break down each one of these for you.

STEP 1: SELECTING A BREED

When it comes to selecting a breed, the first thing you need to consider is *your lifestyle.* Below are some questions to ask yourself so that you can narrow down your search and determine the most suitable breed for you.

LIFESTYLE CONSIDERATIONS

1. Where do you live?

Your living situation matters. Do you live in a downtown apartment or a home in the suburbs? Are you out in the country? Do you have a big yard, a small yard, or no yard at all? Do you have access to hiking trails, or do you live in an urban area?

How much space you have to offer a dog informs the size and energy level of the dog that you should get. Smaller and lower-energy dogs do fine in close quarters, whereas bigger and higher-energy dogs need more room to run.

You should also find out if your apartment, homeowners association, or home insurance plan has any breed restrictions. This could significantly impact your options.

2. Who lives with you?

Do you live alone, have roommates, or are you married with kids? If you do not have kids now, do you plan to have them sometime in the next ten to fifteen years? A dog is a long-term commitment.

What about allergies? Does anyone have allergies to pet dander? Is a low-shedding dog a better option for you? Does anyone have breed preferences?

Planning ahead is key!

Letting everyone weigh in on selecting a puppy will help things go more smoothly in the long run because raising a puppy requires all hands on deck.

3. What does your schedule look like?

Who will be the puppy's primary caretaker and what does that person's schedule look like?

Chances are, *you* are the primary caregiver. So, let me ask you, do you work long hours or short hours? Do you work from home or are you a stay-at-home parent? How much time do you have on a daily basis to invest into your dog's exercise, training, and care?

The average dog needs approximately one hour, every day, of exercise, training, and care. You can double this amount for high-drive dogs, high-energy dogs, and working dogs. A dog owner must always be honest about their schedule and available time before selecting a dog (or even deciding to get one in the first place). Too much dog and too little time is a recipe for disaster!

4. How active are you?

Are you an active person who likes to be outdoors? Do you spend your free time exercising, exploring, and being on the move, or do you prefer a more sedentary lifestyle?

Ideally, you want to select a dog whose energy level matches or is less than yours.

Do not get a high-energy dog in hopes of using that dog to coerce you into going outside and being more active. That kind of plan usually backfires and results in a dog who is restless, pacing, whining, and potentially destructive because their needs are not being met on a regular basis.

I am a high-energy person, and I do best with medium-energy dogs. My dogs are happy to go hiking, biking, and running with me while also being content laying around the house while I get work done.

5. What job do you need this dog to do?

Two all-important questions: Why are you getting a dog, and what is the dog going to do?

Most dogs have a primary job and a secondary job. The primary job is what the dog does most of the time. The secondary job is what the dog does only part of the time.

My dogs are versatile and have four main jobs. They are family dogs, service dogs, protection dogs, and helper dogs for me as a dog trainer. I ask a lot of them, and, in return, I am very careful to select dogs who have the genetic potential for all four jobs. From there, I raise them to excel in all four of their jobs, with family dog being primary and most important.

So, I ask you one more time, what are you getting your dog for? Do you want a family companion, a hunting dog, a working dog, a therapy dog, a service dog, or maybe a sport dog? The job you choose for your dog is what they will be doing most of the time.

Take some time to really think about what you *want* and *need* in a dog.

6. How experienced are you with dogs?

Is this your first dog, or have you had dogs your whole life? How many dogs have you raised? How many have you trained? How successful were you?

Being honest about your personal experience with dogs will help eliminate dogs that may not be a good fit for you. Typically, high-speed dogs and working breeds are more responsibility than most people can handle. The higher the dog's drive, the faster they go and the harder they can be to handle.

Getting a dog is like buying a car. Focus on what you *need* as opposed to what you *want.* A high-drive dog is like a sports car. Do you need a sports car, or are you looking for a daily commuter?

Now, let's talk about breeds!

BREEDS AND BREED GROUPS

There is a huge variety of dog breeds to choose from. In fact, there are over 330 internationally recognized dog breeds. For the sake of simplicity, we are going to focus on breeds recognized within the American Kennel Club (AKC). The AKC recognizes over two hundred different breeds, categorized into seven breed groups. Each breed group contains dogs that are specifically bred for certain traits and drives.

Let's look at each one.

Breed Group #1: Herding

Herding dogs like Australian cattle dogs, border collies, and German shepherds are incredibly intelligent and have the instinctual ability to control the movement of other animals. These dogs require a job because, if left unchecked, their herding instinct can lead to obsessive-compulsive behaviors like chasing cars, biting tires, and herding children!

Breed Group #2: Hound

Hounds, such as beagles, bloodhounds, and coonhounds, have acute sensing powers and phenomenal stamina. They love to work and have lots of energy. Hounds produce a unique baying sound that may not be everyone's cup of tea.

Breed Group #3: Toy

Toy dogs like Chihuahuas and Havanese have big personalities, so do not let their size fool you! When properly socialized, they are quite adaptable and suitable for a wide range of lifestyles. Socialization is key though because they need to be treated like dogs, not accessories.

Breed Group #4: Non-Sporting

Non-sporting dogs are made up of a diverse group of breeds with varying coats and sizes. Some popular breeds include Boston terriers and French bulldogs. Some of the breeds within this group are laid-back while others are energetic and require ample exercise and training.

Breed Group #5: Sporting

Sporting dogs like English springer spaniels, golden retrievers, and Labrador retrievers are active and alert. They are likable and well-rounded companions who are known for their superior instincts in water and woods. Well-bred sporting dogs are great hunting partners and can be wonderful family dogs too, provided their need to work is regularly fulfilled.

Breed Group #6: Terrier

Terriers are feisty and energetic dogs who are bred to hunt and kill. They are spirited animals who usually have a bit of attitude. Terriers require strong-willed owners who know how to work with them and can fulfill their instinctual desires. Boston Terriers do not fit in this breed group because they were bred primarily as a companion dog and not as a working terrier.

Breed Group #7: Working

Working dogs like cane corsos, giant schnauzers, and Saint Bernards were bred to perform jobs like property protection, sled pulling, and water rescue. They are quick to learn, intelligent, and capable. They make solid working companions but can be unsuitable as family pets. Like all dogs, they need proper socialization and training with owners who can handle their size and strength.

Next, let's talk about a fun topic that is mentioned a lot when researching different breeds: drives!

DRIVES

Drives are dogs' subconscious urges that cause them to act a certain way in the presence of particular stimuli. A dog's drive is their *work ethic.* The higher the drive, the more eager the dog is to work.

Dogs have numerous drives that influence their behavior. The five most common drives are prey drive, food drive, hunt drive, pack drive, and defense drive.

Prey Drive

Prey drive (also called "play drive" or "toy drive") is a dog's desire to stalk, chase, and capture prey. Dogs with high prey drive have an overwhelming desire to chase moving objects. This can be toys, leaves, small animals, cars, and other moving things. High-prey-drive dogs need early and consistent training to cap their drive and control their impulses.

Over the years, I have noticed a correlation between prey drive and overall energy. The more prey drive a dog possesses, the more energetic the dog is going to be. Be careful what you wish for!

Food Drive

Food drive is a dog's desire to work for food and can be considered a subcategory of prey drive. Dogs with high food drive love food and will work for any food reward you offer, including kibble. Dogs with high food drive are fun to train because they are motivated to work and learn.

Hunt Drive

Hunt drive is a dog's instinctual impulse to hunt or search for something using their sense of smell, hearing, and/or taste. Dogs with high hunt drive make excellent working dogs and excel in search and rescue, K9 Nose Work, barn hunt, and other arenas.

Pack Drive

Pack drive is a dog's primal need for social contact. Dogs with high pack drive seek out attention, affection, and companionship from people and other animals, especially those within their pack. Dogs with high pack drive tend to make great service dogs, therapy dogs, and emotional support dogs. They generally do not like to be left alone for long periods of time and can become stage-five clingers. Without proper training, they can develop separation anxiety and become destructive in their homes and crates.

Dogs with moderate to high pack drive are usually easy to train because they are eager to please and willing to work hard for their handlers. Dogs with low pack drive can be harder to train because they are independent and self-serving.

Defense Drive

Last but not least is defense. Defense drive is a dog's desire to protect what is theirs: their home, their family, and their possessions. Defense equates to protection but too much defense is not good. Dogs who are highly defensive can be challenging to work with. They pick fight over flight, and, when left unchecked, can become dangerous. Highly defensive dogs are not a good fit for families and need firm but fair handlers who are confident and consistent.

IDEAL DRIVE COMBINATIONS

You might be thinking, *How much drive is right for me?*

Drive is categorized as low, medium, and high.

For family dogs, I recommend medium-drive dogs because they have enough drive to have fun with the family without being overbearing.

For service dogs, and depending on the dog's exact job, I look for medium to high-drive dogs, specifically low to medium defense drive, medium prey or hunt drive, medium to high pack drive, or high food drive.

If you want a lazy couch potato, get a dog with low drives. If you want a hard-working dog, go for high.

I personally prefer medium and high-drive dogs or dogs with high hunt drive because detection and tracking are two of my favorite things to do. My personal dog, Havok, is a high-drive dog while Zoey is medium drive. My protection dogs in training are medium drive.

WHICH BREED GROUP APPEALS TO YOU?

Now that you have a better understanding of drives, tell me: Which group appeals to you most? Which group of dogs matches the temperament and drives for the jobs you have in mind? Write down those breed groups and do more research on them. Study them extensively! Talk with breeders and groomers. Join chat groups. Visit dog shows and never, ever be afraid to ask questions about a breed you have in mind.

The more you learn, the better you will be at picking the right breed for you!

MY FAVORITE BREEDS

You might be wondering, *Which breeds do you recommend?* I am asked this question a lot. Over the years, I have curated a list of my top breeds based on personal experiences training and interacting with them.

My favorite dog breeds for families are: Australian shepherds, Bernese mountain dogs, Cavalier King Charles spaniels, collies, English golden retrievers, English Labrador retrievers, English mastiffs, English springer spaniels, German shepherds, Havanese, Newfoundlands, and standard poodles.

My preferred dog breeds for service work are: German shepherds, golden retrievers, Labrador retrievers, and standard poodles.

WHAT ABOUT DOODLES?

If you do not know what a doodle is, it is a mix between a purebred dog and a poodle. From my experience, I am on the fence when it comes to this specific breed hybrid.

Sometimes with doodles, you get the best of both worlds—a lower-shedding dog that is healthy and has a great temperament. Other times, you get a hodgepodge of genetics and a dog who is unstable, unpredictable, and plagued with health problems.

When looking at doodle breeders, it is important to find a breeder whose focus is on health and temperament as opposed to size and color.

NARROWING DOWN BREEDS

Now that you have done your research on dog breeds, narrow down your list to just one or two breeds before embarking on step two of the puppy selection process. Remember, you can always try additional breeds in the future if you do not find a breeder that suits you.

STEP 2: CHOOSING A BREEDER (OR RESCUE)

Choosing the right breeder (or sourcing your puppy) is just as important as choosing the right breed. Whether you adopt or shop, there is a lot you need to learn. Let's start with breeders.

First realize that purebred does not equal well-bred. There are more bad breeders out there than good ones, and locating a great breeder can feel like searching for a needle in a haystack! I am going to help you sift through breeders so that you can find one that is responsible, ethical, and produces quality puppies.

BLOODLINES

Puppies can inherit behavioral traits like fear and aggression the same way they inherit phenotypes like size, coat, and color. Study bloodlines before picking a breeder and buying a puppy.

When you select a well-bred dog from good bloodlines, you are honestly stacking the deck in your favor.

How do you find a well-bred dog? You start with a reputable breeder!

REPUTABLE BREEDERS

A reputable breeder focuses on producing sound and stable dogs with good drives, good orthopedics, good health, great temperaments, and strong pedigrees. A reputable breeding program that is worth its time, money, and final product can be hard to find.

Here are ten traits all good breeders have in common:

1. Good breeders health test.

Good breeders put their dogs through extensive health testing. This ensures their dogs are genetically sound and are capable of producing healthy puppies with no congenital or predisposed health problems.

Health testing is breed-specific. It can include hip and elbow X-rays, spinal evaluations, cardiac testing, eye exams, DNA panels, and more. Even though it is expensive, all reputable breeders do it.

For a complete list of breed health testing requirements, the Orthopedic Foundation for Animals (OFA) created the Canine Health Information Center (CHIC), where anyone can go online and browse by breed to find specific health screenings recommended for different breeds.

Getting a clean bill of health from the vet does NOT count as health testing.

2. Good breeders title their dogs.

Titling dogs allows breeders to be able to prove that their dogs possess the character traits, drives, structure, and conformation the breed is intended to have. Some titles include show titles in the ring and/or working titles in dog sports such as agility, barn hunt, dock diving, herding, protection sports, and obedience. Know what your breed of choice is known for and look for breeders titling in that particular arena.

In many breeding programs, males are titled whereas females are not titled or have lesser titles than males. This is acceptable and usually depends on that breeder's access to training and trials. Claiming that a dog comes from "champion lines" does not suffice for titling.

If you are looking for a "pet-quality" dog, it is still important to choose a top breeder because you want to get a puppy from a breeding program that checks all the boxes. A well-bred dog is a versatile dog! You do not want faulty genetics.

Keep in mind though that titles do NOT define a dog—genetics does. Titles are simply a testament to the effort and investment the breeder has put into the dog, as well as the dog's abilities.

3. Good breeders breed mature dogs.

Typically, females are bred no sooner than their second heat cycle, and males are bred no sooner than twelve months of age. The majority of breeders wait until their dogs are twenty-four months of age and have passed all health testing requirements before breeding.

Beware of breeders who breed dogs that are less than a year old or more than nine years of age.

4. Good breeders provide pedigrees.

Pedigrees are usually listed on their website, and, when you talk to the breeders, they can tell you about dogs within the pedigrees, what they are known for, the types of dogs they produce, and other interesting details. Good breeders know their dogs' pedigrees, are well informed, and can properly answer any question you may have about them.

Breeders can also tell you about their upcoming breedings, why they picked certain pairings, and what they expect each pairing to produce. In addition, when the puppies go home, they are sent home with registration papers based on their pedigrees. A good breeder will also be able to predict the outcome of a litter based on the genetics of the dogs involved.

I am personally a big fan of repeat breedings. A repeat breeding is when a male and female are bred together again because their past litter turned out successfully.

Watch out for breeders who cannot produce pedigrees on their dogs or promise to send paperwork at a later time. This is usually a red flag and means that their dogs are not registered, which means your puppy will not be registered.

5. Good breeders ask and answer questions.

They are just as eager to get to know you as you are them! Good breeders want to make sure you are a good fit for their program and puppies, and the more they learn about you, the better they are able to pick the perfect puppy for you!

Steer clear of breeders who pressure you into placing a deposit or sending a payment without getting to know you first.

6. Good breeders take excellent care of their dogs.

Their dogs have a great quality of life and live in a clean, well-kept environment. Good breeders happily welcome you onto their property and are proud to show you their dogs.

In some cases, breeders have guardian homes for their females where they live with families and only come back for breeding and whelping. I love the concept of guardian homes because it is a win-win for everyone, especially the dog who gets to be a family dog first and a breeding dog second.

7. Good breeders charge a flat rate for puppies.

They do not charge based on color or size. Some good breeders do vary their price point based on the puppy's temperament, working abilities, or buyer's pick order, but, for the most part, their price is the same regardless of which puppy you choose.

8. Good breeders have solid contracts.

Their contract stipulates which puppy is being purchased and comes with a health guarantee, basic care guidelines, breeding rights, and a first right of refusal clause.

Most reputable breeders sell their dogs on a limited registration basis, meaning the dog cannot be bred and full registration is not given unless the dog passes future health testing and titling requirements as specified by the breeder in the contract.

First right of refusal means if, for any reason, you are unable to keep the purchased puppy, the breeder has the first right to buy back or acquire that dog from you. This is how reputable breeders try to ensure, to the best of their ability, that their dogs do not end up in shelters.

You will not see a well-bred, purebred dog in the shelter. Why? Because well-bred dogs come from reputable breeders and reputable breeders *always* take their dogs back.

9. Good breeders sell puppies at seven weeks of age or older.

Good breeders understand the importance of puppies spending time with their mother and littermates. For this reason, reputable breeders do not sell puppies younger than seven weeks of age. In some cases, breeders wait until their puppies are ten to twelve weeks of age before sending them to their new homes. I love this concept and wish more breeders would adopt it.

Allowing a puppy to spend the first three months with their mom and littermates is so valuable!

Beware of breeders who send five- or six-week-old puppies home with buyers. That is way too soon and can have detrimental effects on that puppy's overall development.

10. Good breeders do not sell littermates to the same household.

They know everything about littermate syndrome and will not sell two puppies to the same household at the same time. Good breeders know this can lead to extreme codependency, anxiety, and stunted social growth for the puppies, not to mention the headaches the family will endure trying to raise two puppies at the same time.

I have worked with a lot of clients who thought it would be fun to buy littermates only to find it was a recipe for disaster. I do not recommend it!

REVIEWING A BREEDER'S WEBSITE

Now that you know how to recognize a good breeder, let me give you my CliffsNotes version of how to quickly review a breeder's website:

- First, head straight for the males (sires) page. Are the male dogs in the breeding program health-tested and titled? If so, look at the females (dams) page next. If not, eliminate the breeder and move on to another breeder.
- On the females page, are the dogs in the breeding program health-tested? This is a requirement. Are they titled? Titles are a bonus. If they are health-tested, stay on the website and look for pedigrees next. If they are not health-tested, eliminate the breeder and move on.
- When looking at pedigrees, do you see health testing and/or titling for dogs three to five generations back within the pedigree? Top breeders only breed from proven, titled, and health-tested lines. You should not see huge gaps in the pedigree where information is missing or unlisted. If everything checks out, click on the warm and fuzzy links next. If it appears the dogs are not health-tested/titled, move on to another breeder.
- The warm, fuzzy links include the website's about page, pictures and videos of the dogs, breeding announcements, reviews, testimonials, and social media. Do you like what you see? Any complaints or problems? It is impossible to please *everyone,* but a good breeder should not have a long list of unhappy buyers.

These are the four key areas I personally look for on a breeder's website. I would like to say that approximately 90 percent of breeders do not pass all four criteria, making it extremely challenging to find a good breeder. You will probably search through a wide variety of breeders before landing on a good one.

Learning to assess a breeder's program from a critical and logical point of view, as opposed to an emotional one, will help you determine if they are reputable or not.

Steer clear of puppy mills, profit-mongering pet stores, backyard breeders, and breeders who are producing dogs solely for size and color. You want a great dog, and that means you need to start with a great puppy. A poorly bred dog can end up having expensive and debilitating health problems, unfixable temperament issues, and other defective issues.

Is adopting a poorly bred dog a risk you are willing to take?

REPUTABLE RESCUES

I am all for rescuing dogs. I have worked with thousands of rescue dogs in my career, and my company has donated more than $60,000 in time and training to rescue groups and nonprofits. I love rescue dogs.

But there is a little more risk involved in rescue because you do not have the same information in regards to the dog's parentage, pedigree, and genetic predispositions for health problems and temperament traits.

If you choose to go the rescue route, make sure you pick a responsible, honest rescue or shelter. Where there is money to be made, there will always be fakes and frauds.

Here are seven quick tips on how to spot a good rescue.

1. Good rescues keep dogs for a minimum of seven days.

This allows the rescue personnel to get to know the dog both physically and mentally prior to adopting the dog out. They do not offer same-day adoptions because a wait period is very important.

2. Good rescues provide information about the dog's history.

This includes basic information such as whether the dog came from a shelter or if the dog was an owner-surrender. If the dog was an owner-surrender, they can provide information regarding the conditions of that situation.

3. Good rescues meet with all human and canine family members first.

This is done in person, unless extenuating circumstances prohibit an in-person meeting.

4. Good rescues provide support after the dog has been adopted.

This includes training advice and trainer referrals and/or medical assistance for issues popping up shortly after the adoption.

5. Good rescues take dogs back no matter what.

If the dog exhibits behavioral problems and cannot be kept by the new owner(s), or if the person changes their mind, the rescue will always take the dog back.

6. Good rescues do not always require a fenced-in yard.

They understand that fences alone do not set dogs up for success and can sometimes give owners an excuse to be lazy and not exercise their dog.

7. Good rescues typically do not adopt two dogs to the same household at the same time.

They want each dog to receive the proper amount of time and attention to help the adoption be a success!

BOTTOM LINE

Whether you choose to adopt or shop, do so responsibly. Together, we can help put an end to irresponsible breeding, backyard "greeders," and puppy mills.

STEP 3: PICKING A PUPPY

Picking a puppy is a big responsibility. I would say that, in a litter of eight puppies, only one or two of them might be the right fit for your home and family. Since that is the case, let's discuss some important considerations when picking a puppy and then dive deep into temperament testing, a topic that most highly skilled dog trainers, like myself, love exploring.

ADDING A PUPPY TO YOUR PACK

If you already have dogs and are looking to add a puppy to your pack, choose wisely. You want to get a puppy that is a good fit with your current pack.

Dominant alpha dogs do not get along with other dominant alpha dogs. Submissive dogs do best with confident, laid-back dogs. If one could not guess it, male dogs get along best with female dogs and vice versa.

If any of your current dogs have behavioral issues, sort those out first before bringing home a puppy. Your new puppy is going to model your pack's behavior—and like a brand-new marriage, that is for better or for worse!

THE BEST TIME OF YEAR TO GET A PUPPY

In my opinion, spring is the best time of year to get a puppy because it gives a dog owner time to begin training at home before venturing out into public for field trips. Summertime is perfect for socializing puppies because people are out enjoying the nice weather.

MALES VERSUS FEMALES

Now that you have selected a breed and chosen a breeder, the breeder will usually ask if you want a male or a female and will assist you in choosing the right litter for your needs. If you are unsure whether you want a male or a female, I have some suggestions that might help you. Here are some general differences that I have noticed between males and females.

Male dogs are generally:	Female dogs are generally:
Better with women	better with men
forgiving of mistakes	unforgiving of mistakes, hold grudges
tolerant of corrections	sensitive to corrections
harder to handle	easier to handle
slower learners	quicker learners
slower to mature	faster to mature
less in tune with handler emotions	more in tune with handler emotions

Female dogs tend to be better family dogs and service dogs, whereas male dogs tend to be better working dogs and sport dogs. Keep in mind though, these are just generalizations. I personally tend to prefer male dogs. My heart dog is a male, but my soul dog is a female!

A heart dog is the dog of your heart – the one that feels like it was *made for you.* It is usually the dog you connect with more deeply than any other. The bond often builds gradually, and it feels natural, constant, and intensely personal. A heart dog is your best friend and is irreplaceable. A soul dog is a once-in-a-lifetime, soulmate dog. The connection feels spiritual—like your souls have always been connected, maybe even across lifetimes (for those who believe in that). It often comes with an overwhelming sense of *knowing*—as if the dog was always meant to find you. A soul dog is a part of who you are.

PICK OF THE LITTER

When I put down a deposit on a litter, I want to have the first or second pick of the gender I have chosen because getting pick of the litter is ideal. Second pick is acceptable if it is a large litter. I will pass on a litter and wait for the next one if the first and second picks are already taken.

TEMPERAMENT TESTING

Some experts say that when it comes to picking a puppy from a well-bred litter, it does not matter which puppy you pick.

I disagree!

Puppies are individuals just like people. Some puppies have more energy and drive while others have less. Some puppies are confident and outgoing while others are shy and reserved. It is important to look at each puppy's temperament when it comes to picking out the right puppy for you.

Keep in mind: some breeders choose puppies for their buyers because they know their puppies well and usually do a great job matching puppies with families.

I like to personally evaluate puppies myself so that way I can compare my "pick puppy" to the breeder's pick puppy and compare notes.

Many people are intimidated by the idea of temperament testing. Do not be! It is easier to do than you think.

Ideally, the best age for temperament testing is forty-nine days old (give or take a day). By eight weeks old, puppies might be in a "fear period," which could skew results. (We will discuss fear periods in Chapter 9.)

Over the years, I have crafted a proven seven-step temperament test, and I would love to share it with all of you! Here is what I do and look for when I evaluate a litter of puppies. Much of this guidance can also be applied to the rescue scenario.

MY SEVEN-STEP TEMPERAMENT TEST

Pre-Testing Instructions

- Testing should be done in a new or relatively unfamiliar environment.
- Ask to see only the puppies you will be choosing from (e.g., only males or only females).
- Ask the breeder to not feed the puppies prior to the test (hungry is good).
- Take notes or ask someone to take notes on your behalf.
- Have the following props on hand:
    - a notepad
    - puppy food
    - two new sights (e.g., an umbrella and a cooking pot)
    - two new sounds (e.g., pan lids and a vitamin container)
    - a small dog toy

You can access this test on our website blog (www.valork9academy-online.com) or by scanning the QR code below.

Now, let's go through each of the seven steps!

Step 1: Observe the Litter

Ask the breeder to put all of the puppies you will be evaluating in a whelping box or fenced area. Observe them from a distance, without approaching or distracting them. When doing this, look for obvious temperament traits. Which puppy is dominant and which one is submissive? Which puppy plays rough and which one is gentle? Which puppy is loud, which one is quiet, and which one is right in between?

How a puppy acts with its littermates reflects how that puppy will act in your home. Find the puppy or puppies you like the best, based on the job(s) you have in mind, and ask the breeder to identify those puppies' collar colors. Be sure to write them down.

Step 2: Approach the Litter

While the puppies are contained, walk up to them to see how they react. The ones that run up to you and bark excitedly are going to be your more confident, dominant, and outgoing puppies.

The puppies that hide in the back are going to be your more shy and reserved puppies, some of them also being a bit fearful.

The puppies that sit in the middle of the room and study you as chaos unfolds around them—I like to call them the middle-of-the-road puppies—are my favorite. When I am looking for family dogs, active companions, and service dogs, they are my front-runners because they tend to grow up to be confident, laid-back dogs who are a good fit for most homes and families.

Step 3: Assess Pack Drive

At this step, select one puppy and complete steps 3–7 with it before switching to another puppy.

Put the puppy down in the middle of the floor in an open area and walk away from it. Does the puppy follow you? Does it wander off? Does it appear to be indifferent?

The puppy that follows you, jumps on you, and just wants to be with you has high pack drive. The puppy that doesn't follow you, ignores you, or wanders off has lower pack drive and is more independent.

Step 4: Handle the Puppy

Pick up the puppy and pet it all over. Touch its ears, mouth, back, and paws. How does it react? A confident puppy who has had a good start in life will enjoy being petted all over. A nervous or uncomfortable puppy will be stiff or tense and will not appear to enjoy being handled.

If the puppy enjoys being handled, try putting it on its back. Cradle the puppy in your arms and put your hand on its chest. Does the puppy fight you a lot, a little, or not at all?

I like puppies who are confident enough to fight a little but settle in quickly. I like puppies who are comfortable being uncomfortable because that tells me they will adapt and be easy to work with and handle. Puppies who are stiff or cry endlessly on their backs are anxious and lack confidence. Puppies who fight and bite over and over tend to be more dominant and will need a firm handler.

Step 4 tells you a lot about the puppy you may be about to purchase and raise.

Step 5: See How They React to New Sights

Put the puppy down and pick up one of your props, either the pot or the umbrella. Set it down a few feet away from the puppy and gauge the puppy's reaction. Does the puppy ignore it or go check it out? Both reactions are signs of a confident, stable puppy.

A puppy who panics, runs away, hides, or does not come back lacks confidence and has poor nerves. That is not a puppy you want!

If the puppy was confident and handled the first sight well, present the second sight and see if the reaction is the same. You want to see consistent confidence, a sign of a good puppy!

Step 6: See How They React to New Sounds

Pick up one of your sound props. I like to use a vitamin container first. Shake it loudly and then set it on the ground to see how the puppy reacts. You want to see a confident puppy who is willing to go and inspect the sound-maker, even if they may have been startled at first.

If all goes well with the first prop, move to the second prop. I like to use a pan lid. Drop it about five feet away from the puppy. How does the puppy react?

Your assessment here will be similar to Step 5. Look for neutral or curious behavior. Extremely fearful puppies are removed from the list of potentials.

Step 7: Assess Trainability

It is time for the final test item! You want to see how *trainable* the puppy will be and how strong their drive is.

Take a piece of the puppy's food and present it to them. Does the puppy eagerly grab it? What happens if you move the food a few inches? Does the puppy follow it and continue trying to eat it?

If so, this is a puppy with high food drive. The higher the food drive, the more motivated the puppy is and the easier training will be. If the puppy is not interested in the food, they have lower food drive. This can be corrected through existential feeding (working for food), but the more food drive you see at this age, the better off you will be when it comes time for training.

Now, try the toy. Present the toy and flick it around in front of the puppy. A puppy with high prey drive will chase the toy, grab it, and shake it. The more interested the puppy is in the toy, the higher the drive. A less interested puppy has lower prey drive.

Prey drive is something that usually increases with age, so take that into consideration when deciding how much drive you want to see at this age in the puppy.

Do steps 3 through 7 with each eligible puppy. When you have finished testing, review your notes.

AFTER TESTING

After testing, put the puppies away and chat with the breeder about your findings. Does the breeder agree or disagree with your assessment? Sometimes puppies have bad days and do not test as well as they could or should. If the breeder's top pick for you did not test well one day, try testing again the next day or the day after.

What happens if you cannot decide? If you like more than one puppy, bring them out together and put them on the ground. Observe them. Which puppy is more active? Which puppy is more vocal? Which one is dominant? Which one is submissive? Seeing all the puppies together might make your decision a little bit easier.

MY TWO CENTS

When all else fails, pick the middle-of-the-road puppy—the puppy who has decent drives, but is not over the top, and is the best fit for most homes, including yours.

Avoid fearful puppies and overly aggressive and dominant puppies.

If you are not confident going into the test on your own, consult a trainer or breeder. When I personally evaluate puppies for clients, I look at tiny behaviors like decision-making processes while studying their every move. I have a trained, unbiased eye, and I realize how invaluable experience is when it comes to puppy selection.

Good breeders know their puppies and will help you pick the right one.

If no puppies in the litter check the boxes for you, move on, roll your deposit, and wait for a future litter. You will be glad you did! I have personally rolled deposits on more than one occasion because the right puppy is always worth the wait!

Chapter Summary

Getting a puppy is a big responsibility that should not be taken lightly. It takes countless hours of researching, probing, and searching to select a breed, choose a breeder (or rescue), and pick a puppy.

By doing the legwork first and remaining objective throughout the process, you can end up with your dream puppy, a puppy that is perfect for you!

Finding the right puppy is the first step on the road to success.

Module 1

7-Step Temperament Test

Step 1: Observe the Litter

From a distance, what do you see?
Notes:

Step 2: Approach the Litter

How do the puppies react when you approach?

Complete Steps 3-7 below with one puppy at a time.

Step 3: Pack Drive

Put the puppy down and walk away. What does s/he do?

Module 1

7-Step Temperament Test

Step 4: Handling

Pick up the puppy and pet him/her all over. How does s/he react?

Step 5: New Sights

Put the puppy down and set down a new sight by him/her. How does the puppy react? If all goes well, use the second sight.

Step 6: New Sounds

Make noise with one of the sound props. How does the puppy react? If all goes well, use the second sound too.

Step 7: Food and Prey Drives

How much does the puppy want food? Will the puppy chase a toy?

Additional Notes:

Testing complete! Time to review your notes and write additional notes here.

2.

PREPARING FOR YOUR PUPPY

"By failing to prepare, you are preparing to fail."
—Otto von Bismarck

You've picked your puppy. Let's get ready for their arrival.

In this chapter, I discuss what to buy and how to prepare your home and family for your new puppy. These topics will include training equipment, food, bones, treats, toys, and crate information. I also cover puppy-proofing tips and guidelines for a family meeting.

This chapter is short and sweet.

TRAINING EQUIPMENT

I am a firm believer that, when it comes to training equipment, you get what you pay for. I have Amish leather leashes and collars that I purchased over a decade ago at Vohne Liche Kennels and still use them today!

Quality gear costs more up front, but it lasts for years to come, so try to make it a worthwhile investment!

I am putting training equipment into two categories: essential items and optional extras. You can buy what you need or buy what you want.

For your convenience and to help you pick the correct items, everything in this chapter is available on my Amazon Storefront, www.amazon.com/shop/dogtraineramy, in the Puppy Head Start section.

I receive a small commission from each item sold, so I thank you in advance for your consideration.

ESSENTIAL ITEMS

1. SLIP LEAD

First things first—you need a slip lead. A slip lead is a combination leash and collar that is adjustable to any neck size. From day one, I use a slip lead with every single dog I train because it truly is an essential piece of equipment.

My favorite slip lead is the Mendota 3/8-inch-by-six-foot slip lead. It is soft on the hands, easy to use, and compact enough to fit in your coat pocket. This certain slip lead is made of waterproof, long-lasting, multi-filament polypropylene rope with metal hardware and a leather stopper. On top of that, Mendota slip leads are handmade in the good ole US of A!

Avoid slip leads that are:

- bulky
- made out of bungee material
- thinner than 3/8 inch

- thicker than 1/2 inch
- designed as a martingale show lead

2. TREAT POUCH

A treat pouch is another must-have item because it gives you quick access to kibble during your training sessions. I like a low-profile treat pouch that snaps shut and fits snugly against my body.

PetSafe makes a great treat pouch. It is waterproof, stain-resistant, machine-washable, and has a hinge on it that helps it stay open and shut when desired. It comes in two sizes: standard and mini. Get the standard one for adults or the mini for kids.

3. LONG LINE

Back when I was a newbie K9 handler, I used a black nylon long line. Boy, was that a mistake! Nylon cuts into your hands and, when wet, it is heavy, stinky, and hard to clean. I lost that long line during nighttime tracking training and it is probably for the better!

The best long line is made out of BioThane material. I like fifteen-foot long lines with a small, lightweight, metal clasp.

4. HARNESS

You will need a good puppy harness—one with a V-chest plate on front to evenly distribute pressure from pulling and a ring on the back (top) to clip your long line to.

I would also consider getting an adjustable harness that can grow with your puppy. If you can find a harness that allows for patches, that is ideal. Buy a “Do Not Pet” Velcro patch because you will use it later on when your puppy is older and needs to work on manners and neutrality in public.

Avoid:

- no-pull harnesses

- harnesses with a front clip
- heavy and bulky harnesses
- non-adjustable harnesses

5. PLACE BED

A place bed is a raised bed with defined edges. Your puppy will be trained to stand up, sit, or lay on it, but to also not get off it until given permission to do so. Place bed training helps foster independence without using a crate while also teaching good house manners.

The place bed is a training tool and different from an orthopedic or fluffy dog bed.

Kuranda makes the best place beds in the country. They are made in the USA and last a lifetime. When shopping for your puppy's place bed, invest in one that has an aluminum frame, anodized corners, and forty-ounce heavy-duty vinyl. They are easy to clean and chew-proof—although, with how we train, chewing will not be an issue!

Purchase the size that will best fit your dog's length or weight as an adult. When measuring length, go from tip of nose to base of tail. When in doubt, size up.

Place bed suggestions (will vary by overall length of dog):

Max. length 21" or 20 pounds	Choose 25" by 18" bed
Max. length 25" or 35 pounds	Choose 30" by 20" bed
Max. length 31" or 50 pounds	Choose 35" by 23" bed
Max. length 36" or 75 pounds	Choose 40" by 25" bed
Max. length 40" or 90 pounds	Choose 44" by 27" bed

My preferred place bed size is the 40" by 25" bed. It can be used for small, medium, and large-sized dogs and even fits my large German

Shepherds (though they would be more comfortable on a larger bed for long-term use).

6. CRATE

You need a crate. This is nonnegotiable! Good puppy training entails crate training.

When it comes to crates, there are two primary crate materials available: plastic and wire. I'm going to list the pros and cons of each and then share my preferences.

Plastic Crate Considerations

Pros	Cons
Provides a den-like atmosphere for dogs	Does not fold up
Covered top/sides are comforting for puppies	Not adjustable in size
Can cover with towel to reduce visual stimuli	May have to buy more than one
Plastic bottom is quiet when puppy moves	

Wire Crate Considerations

Pros	Cons
Usually comes with an adjustable inner wall	Cannot be covered easily with a towel
Tray is easy to remove for cleaning	Puppies can pull towels in and ingest them
Crate collapses for travel	Difficult to clean wire sides if puppy poops
	Nails are loud on crate tray bottom

I use a plastic crate first for young puppies—during the first eight weeks or so of crate training and potty training—then I upgrade to a wire crate. My favorite plastic crate is by Petmate but I also like Midwest wire crates.

Consider getting a bonus crate for your vehicle so that you do not have to move the crate to and from your house for field trips with your puppy. When purchasing a car crate, if you can afford it, get a crate that has been crash-tested for safety.

K9 Kennel Boss makes a lightweight, collapsible crate that is affordable and crash-tested for safety. You can enter the code VALOR10 at checkout for a discount.

For your puppy's first crate, you will want a crate that is just big enough for them to stand up, turn around, and lay down in. You do not want a crate that is too big or it will hinder your crate-training and potty-training progress.

7. PUPPY TOY

I personally buy a small puppy toy to use for the first few weeks. It is something lightweight that you can use to play with your puppy and tire them out in the evenings before bedtime when it is dark out, you are tired and ready for bed, and your puppy is not quite ready to sleep yet. This toy does not need to be tough, durable, or expensive. It will not be used for very long because your puppy will quickly outgrow it and playtime will soon become more structured. Caution: make sure the toy is small but not a choking hazard.

OPTIONAL EXTRAS

1. CLICKER

The best clickers are easy to press, make a good sound, and include a wristband. I like the Starmark Pro-Training Clicker Deluxe. I order my Valor K9 Academy clickers through the same manufacturer and have used them for years.

2. FLAT COLLAR

When it comes to collars, there are a plethora of options out there. I like BioThane and leather collars with metal buckles. You want a simple but hardy collar that will not fall off, loosen on its own over time, or break easily.

Avoid collars that:

- are made out of nylon
- have plastic components
- clasp together

3. ID TAG

Puppies need to wear identification tags in case they get lost so that the person who finds them can call and return your puppy. I do not recommend purchasing noisy tags that constantly jingle because your poor puppy will never get any peace and quiet.

My favorite ID tag is a flat panel that attaches directly to the collar or a phone number sewn into the collar itself.

4. TUG TOYS

If you have a working breed puppy or a puppy with medium to high prey drive, I highly recommend investing in a quality tug toy. This will be a great relationship builder for you and your puppy and a great outlet for excess energy. A tug that is ten to twelve inches long with handles on both ends is ideal. I highly recommend RedLine K-9's tug for its durability.

Beware of squeaky toys. They create conflict by getting the dog excited and in a high prey/chase/kill state of mind. Squeakers make it harder to play nicely with a dog who is very amped up and can make it more difficult to teach good play skills. Less excitement is key when it comes to puppy play dog—not more.

5. BALLS

Do not buy tennis balls for your puppy. The felt on the ball wears down enamel and can damage your puppy's teeth over time. The best ball is made out of rubberized material. Chuckit! makes a rubber ball that's fairly durable against popping.

Be sure to select a ball that is larger than your puppy's trachea. Balls can be a choking hazard, so getting a large enough ball is important. Size up as your puppy grows and throw away balls that become too small.

6. FLIRT POLE

A flirt pole is like a fishing pole with a line and toy on the other end. It is a great way to build your puppy's drive and tire out your puppy. Squishy Face, a small Florida-based company, makes a great flirt pole. I have had mine for almost a decade now and it is still going strong! When the toy on the end wears out, you can also purchase a replacement without replacing the entire pole.

7. INTERACTIVE TOYS

Interactive toys like KONGs provide mental stimulation for your puppy. They are great for busy days, bad weather, and days when life is simply too busy to work with your dog the way you want to.

Get a KONG that is larger than your puppy's trachea and size up as needed, or buy a very large size to begin with.

When it comes to interactive toys, look for something that you can put food inside of. My dogs' favorite interactive toys are the KONG Wobbler and the Starmark Treat Dispensing Chew Ball. They are on my Amazon list! (And if all of this is new to you, do not worry because I am going to teach you how to properly stuff KONGs and interactive toys. They are a lot of fun!)

Do not buy:

- laser pointers

- automatic ball throwers
- automatic treat dispensers
- other such toys

These products promote neurotic and obsessive-compulsive behavior.

8. IMMUNE SUPPORT AND STOOL SUPPORT SUPPLEMENTS

I recommend purchasing Vibactra Immune Support and Kochi Free Healthy Stools supplements. These tinctures will help boost your puppy's immune system and solidify their stools to prevent accidents in the crate. Be sure to refrigerate the supplements after opening.

TRAINING COLLARS

Do not buy correction collars, such as prong collars, e-collars, or bark collars for your puppy. Correction collars should never be used on puppies under six months of age because they can create confusion and superstitious associations and stunt confidence building.

There is a time and place for training collars. When dogs are six months of age and older, and understand what is expected of them, they are ready for a training collar. You will not need one now for your puppy.

EQUIPMENT SUMMARY

This is only a summary; there may be additional equipment needs that arise as you train your puppy. If you have already purchased equipment that is on my no-no lists of things to avoid, I kindly ask you to please throw those things away and start fresh. Having the right equipment makes a big difference when it comes to good training!

Next, let's talk about food and nutrition!

FOOD AND NUTRITION

I wholeheartedly believe in implementing a balanced, fresh, raw diet with all of my dogs. With puppies, since I use food as a reward for training and because they lack the enzymes to digest uncooked food, I prefer to feed them kibble.

The puppy kibble I carry in my retail section is Farmina N&D Ancestral Grain Lamb and Blueberry Puppy Food, and it is the best kibble money can buy. It is a European product with premium ingredients and grass-fed protein. I also like The Honest Kitchen. If you are looking for a more budget-friendly food, my top three recommendations are Fromm (family-owned from Wisconsin), NutriSource, and Nulo.

If you want to save time, take my advice and buy Farmina. If you are on the fence or wanting to shop around, here is some information to help guide you in your decision-making when picking out food for your new best friend.

READING A LABEL

Do not look at the front of the dog food bag. Since the Food and Drug Administration (FDA) does not regulate what is on the front of food bags, companies can make any claims they want, even if they are not true. Beware of catchy words like "holistic" and "organic"! They are meant to lure you in.

Instead, read the label on the back of the bag. That is where the FDA requires honesty and transparency. Dog food ingredients in the United States are listed in descending order of pre-cooked weight. The first five ingredients typically constitute a significant portion of the recipe.

Look for the following ingredients:

- deboned protein
- dehydrated protein
- whole animal protein
- named organ meats (e.g., beef liver, chicken gizzards)

- protein meal (e.g., chicken meal)
- animal fat
- protein oil

Avoid these ingredients:

- by-products (aka slaughterhouse waste)
- non-specific meals (e.g., poultry meal)
- anonymous meat ingredients (e.g., dehydrated fish)
- bone meal (e.g., cornmeal, pea protein)
- food coloring dyes
- animal by-products

PROTEIN, FAT, FILLERS, AND GRAINS

Protein is the most expensive ingredient in dog food. Since dogs are carnivores, they need as much of it as they can get. Quality kibble lists protein as the first and second ingredients with additional proteins in the top ten ingredients.

In addition to protein, puppies need fat because it contains double the energy that protein does. Always be on the lookout for animal fats in the ingredients lineup.

What dogs do not need are large amounts of fillers, grains, or carbohydrates. They do not process carbs like we do. They have no nutritional value and, worse yet, they take a toll on their digestive system.

To figure out how much of a kibble is carbohydrates, look for the Guaranteed Analysis label on the food. Add up the protein, fat, fiber, and moisture contents, then add in ash (if it is not listed, assume it is 6 percent). (Ash in dog food represents the mineral content left after the food is burned, which includes essential minerals like calcium and phosphorus that are important for your dog's health. It is not harmful and is a necessary part of a balanced diet, although too much ash can lead to health issues.)

Subtract your number from one hundred. The number you end up with is how much of the food is carbohydrates and fillers. Ideally, you want around 30 percent filler foods or less.

WHICH PROTEIN IS BEST?

Hooved animals are generally the best, most natural protein source for dogs. This list includes lamb, beef, boar, venison, and elk. Dogs can eat pig too, but I tend to stay away from feeding pig meat to my dogs. Pork can pose health risks for dogs, particularly if it is processed or undercooked, as it may carry parasites like trichinella and can lead to digestive issues. Additionally, processed pork products are high in fat and salt, which can be harmful to dogs' health.

If your dog has a food intolerance, it is most likely an intolerance to chicken. If you feed chicken to your dog and notice that they seem itchy, eliminate chicken and see if that helps! (When in doubt, consult your veterinarian.)

I recommend starting your puppy on lamb, beef, venison, or elk as opposed to chicken or turkey. Fish is a good alternative protein source as well.

IS GRAIN-FREE BETTER?

Long story short, no. If you look into it, you will see that going grain-free was a trend that was backed by opinions and not actual science. To date and to my personal knowledge, there is zero research supporting a grain-free diet. On the contrary, the FDA unearthed some information back in 2018/2019 that linked dilated cardiomyopathy (DCM) in dogs with certain grain-free foods.

My philosophy for me and my dogs is "everything in moderation." I feed my dogs grain-in and grain-free kibble in training, then place them on a balanced, fresh, raw diet—as nature intended—as soon as puppy training wraps up.

KIBBLE SIZE

Whichever kibble you choose, make sure the kibble itself is a decent size. For a medium to large-breed puppy, a kibble that is approximately the size of your pinky fingernail is good. Anything smaller causes problems when it falls out of your hand and onto the ground. You want your dog's focus on you—not the floor!

When I feed a medium to large-sized dog my suggested Farmina puppy food, I like to start out with the mini size for the first bag then upgrade to the medium/maxi size.

FEEDING PORTIONS AND TRAINING REWARDS

Use the feeding guidelines on the back of your dog food bag as a starting point. If your puppy eats three cups a day, set that aside in Ziploc bags or containers. Use this kibble for training throughout the day, pulling from your pre-measured amount. This ensures your puppy gets the right amount of food while keeping training consistent and effective.

If your puppy is overweight or underweight, adjust the portions as needed.

TREATS

I never use dog treats in puppy training because I utilize the concept of *existential feeding*, which means that every piece of food the dog eats is earned. No freebies! This increases the value of food for the dog and creates enough motivation that I do not need to up the ante by using treats.

If you are willing to follow my book, I guarantee you will experience the same success with your dog. An owner can purchase treats if they want to, but there is a good possibility you are not going to need them. If you do buy treats, pay close attention to the ingredients and avoid excess sugars and carbohydrates.

I only use treats for service dog training and when I do, I use BilJac liver treats. They are stinky and non-crumbly, and dogs love them!

BONES

My favorite bones for dogs are:

- yak/Himalayan chews
- antlers from deer or elk
- marrow bones
- bully sticks

Avoid rawhides, plastic bones, and rubber bones. They are a choking hazard and can cause digestive distress and intestinal blockage if swallowed.

Also, do not waste your money on dental chews. A raw meaty bone will do the trick when it comes to cleaning your puppy's teeth.

VITAMINS

A good vitamin goes a long way in making sure your pup is getting the nutrients and minerals they need. I like NuVet Labs products—their green bottle (NuVet Plus) and blue bottle (NuJoint Plus)—and have been giving these vitamins to my dogs for years.

To order vitamins for your dog, go to www.nuvet.com/45459 or use my purchase code (45459) at checkout. I receive a small commission from each purchase, so I greatly thank you in advance!

BOTTOM LINE

Do your homework! Nutrition matters. Look into the options that are available to you and ask for help if you need it. Shop small whenever possible and support local, family-owned businesses.

For more information on food and nutrition, go to Chapter 13 (Health and Wellness).

PUPPY-PROOFING YOUR HOME

I remember being pregnant with my daughter Emma. It was such an exciting time! In preparation for her arrival, Justin and I spent countless hours shopping for all the cutest stuff and setting up her nursery. When it was done, we sat in the rocking chair and dreamed of the day we would bring her home.

I hope you feel the same level of joy and enthusiasm about your puppy. Bringing home a puppy is a grand adventure! But keep in mind that puppies are like toddlers. They are super mobile and ready to get into things.

You do not need to radically change your home, but there are a few things you should do to puppy-proof the main rooms of your home. In my house, these rooms include the foyer, laundry room, kitchen, living room, and personal office.

Here are four puppy-proofing tips for you.

PUPPY-PROOFING TIPS

1. PICK THINGS UP OFF THE FLOOR.

Having a neat and tidy home will prevent your puppy from getting into things they should not be getting into. Keep things off the floor and out of the way—including plants!

2. MOVE FRILLY RUGS.

Rugs that are low profile without fringes are fine. Rugs that are fluffy and frilly need to be removed for now. Puppies will chew anything that looks fun or is within reach. Choose your battles. Avoid problems by preventing them!

3. PUT AWAY KID TOYS.

Puppies do not know the difference between dog toys and kid toys initially. Put away all kid toys and simply remove temptation. Kids take it personally when puppies grab their toys. We want to foster a healthy relationship from the initial introduction. That means respecting each other's things!

4. PUT AWAY DOG TOYS.

Dogs should not have 24/7 access to their toys. It is unnecessary and creates added stimulation in the house. My dog toys are kept in the garage, inside a drawer, where they cannot access them. Any time we play with toys, I get the toy, then engage my dog, not the other way around! My dog does not get the toy then entice me to play. I am the leader! I control access to toys.

SETTING UP THE CRATE

WHERE TO PUT THE CRATE

Where are you going to put the crate? The best place for the crate is a low-traffic room, such as a guest bedroom, office, or laundry room. I use my oversized laundry room, which is next to the back door where I take puppies in and out for potty breaks. If you do not have a low-traffic room available, a closet or bathroom will suffice.

I do not recommend putting your puppy's crate in your bedroom. It is important for your puppy to have their own space, independent of you, to help prevent separation anxiety and encourage rest and relaxation.

I prefer to use a room with tile or vinyl flooring, as opposed to rugs or carpeting, in case the puppy has an accident in the crate. A quick clean-up makes your life easier.

PUTTING TOGETHER THE CRATE

If you are using a plastic create, set it up so the door opens *away* from the side your puppy will heel on. For example, if your puppy will be heeling on your left side, position the crate so the door swings from left to right when opening. This way, the door opens away from your puppy during crate drills, creating cleaner entries and exits and reinforcing impulse control later on in training.

Pro tip: If you have a plastic crate, you do not need to put all the screws in. Just one screw on either side of the door, one on each side of the crate, and one in the back (five screws total) will do the trick. This makes for an easier tear-down and clean-up in case your puppy has an accident.

TIPS FOR CRATE TRAINING

To set yourself up for success with crate training, you will need four things:

1. WHITE NOISE

You will need to provide white noise for your puppy to drown out any activity from surrounding rooms. Ideally, the white noise is a fan or noise machine. My laundry room has a built-in ceiling fan that I can turn on with the flick of a switch.

2. TOWEL ON TOP

If you are using a plastic crate, find a towel, sheet, or blanket to cover the crate with. I like to use an oversized bath towel because it provides good coverage without causing the puppy to heat up in the crate.

Wire crates are hard to cover. You cannot cover them with a towel or blanket because puppies pull them through. Try using cardboard boxes or something else flat that cannot be chewed.

3. TOWEL INSIDE

Place a towel inside the crate that covers the surface area of the crate bottom. This towel will provide comfort to your puppy and will soak up any accidents your puppy has in the crate. I use older towels that I am willing to throw away in case of an accident. Do not use a towel with rips and tears in it. If the towel has a tag, remove it so your puppy does not chew it. I do not recommend putting a mat or bed in the crate with your puppy—it is likely to be chewed or damaged in the early weeks of crate training.

If your puppy ever chews on the towel in the crate, take it out immediately and do not put another one back in. Privilege revoked!

4. BONE INSIDE

Put a low-value bone, such as an antler, in the crate so your puppy has something to chew on. Never put toys in the crate. The crate is a place to relax and decompress, not play.

The reason I recommend an antler for the crate and not a bully stick is because bully sticks are nutrient-dense, which can cause diarrhea in young puppies. Bully sticks are generally only fine if they are only chewed on for five or ten minutes at a time, whereas antlers can be chewed on for hours without causing digestive upset.

Now that you have puppy-proofed your home and your crate is ready, it is time to get your family ready!

PREPARING YOUR FAMILY

Before your new puppy comes home, everyone in the family needs to be on the same page in regard to raising, training, and caring for the puppy. You need to discuss a handful of key topics.

PRIMARY CARETAKER

First things first, who is going to be the puppy's primary caretaker? This is the person who is responsible for pottying, training, and overall caring for the puppy. Remember, if everyone is doing it, then no one is doing it. There needs to be one responsible person—preferably an adult—who assumes full responsibility for the puppy. This is most likely who the puppy is going to be the most bonded to.

KIDS' ROLES

But what about the kids, you ask? Kids can and should be involved in helping with the puppy. For the first few weeks when the puppy is very young, your kids will be less involved. This is because the puppy is biting and jumping a lot and does not have much training.

I think it is best to get the puppy's training underway first then slowly integrate the kids into the puppy's everyday life. Once the pup has better manners, your kiddos can help out more.

Doing things right means doing things slowly and in a controlled manner. There is a time and a place for everything. Let the first month of work fall upon the shoulders of the primary caretaker. Then, once you have the puppy under control, let the kids be more involved. They can enjoy the fruits of your labor!

My three-year-old daughter Emma training the dogs, circa 2023.

LATE-NIGHT POTTY BREAKS

If you are the puppy's primary caretaker, it is important for you to get some sleep. This means delegating responsibility, if possible. When your puppy needs to go potty in the middle of the night, can your spouse or someone else in the household take your puppy out for you?

My husband Justin lets puppies out for me every other night for the first month. It is a big help!

DAYTIME POTTY BREAKS

The same goes for daytime potty breaks. Your puppy will not be able to "hold it" for eight hours while you are at work. If you work away from home, make sure you have a plan in place for potty breaks.

HOUSE RULES

Imagine if someone you did not know quite well was coming to live with you for several months. Upon their arrival, you would probably sit down with them, discuss expectations, show them their room, discuss a plan for meals and clean-up, and ask them to keep the noise down at night, take their shoes off in the house, and close the toilet lid. Common things like that! Things that would help make their extended visit pleasant by getting everyone on the same page.

Clear communication is key!

Dogs deserve the same communication. Puppies need house rules. As a family, you need to decide what your puppy's house rules are. Write them down on a piece of paper and put that paper on the fridge as a daily reminder.

Here are some of the house rules I have for my dogs:

HOUSE RULES FOR DOGS

1. No jumping.

Not today. Not tomorrow. Not ever. Do not jump on me. Do not jump on anyone else.

2. No biting.

Not today. Not tomorrow. Not ever. Do not bite me, even during play, or anyone else.

3. No begging.

Do not beg for food. Do not beg for attention. Do not be obnoxious.

4. No playing in the house.

Do not play in the house. You are expected to be calm in the house. Play is for outside. (There are a few exceptions to this rule.)

5. Stay off furniture.

Stay off furniture unless you're invited to come up. If you are, lay calmly. When I tell you to get off, do so immediately.

6. Move out of my way.

When I walk through a room, move out of my way. I will not walk around you or step over you. I am the pack leader. Move!

7. An open door is not an invitation.

When I open a door (front door, back door, sliding door, etc.), you cannot go through unless I give you permission to do so. The same goes for gates.

8. Get out of the kitchen.

When I am cooking food, get out of the kitchen and stay out of the kitchen.

Chapter Summary

Getting ready for your new puppy is fun! By preparing ahead of time, you will be ready to jump right in when your new puppy arrives.

Module 2

Training Equipment

Essential Items

- Slip Lead
- Treat Pouch
- Long Line
- Harness
- Place Bed
- Crate
- Puppy Toy

Food

- Kibble
- Chew Bones
- Vitamins

Optional Extras

- Clicker
- Flat Collar
- ID Tag
- Tug Toy
- Ball
- Flirt Pole
- Interactive Toys
- Vibactra Immune Support
- Kochi Free Healthy Stools

3.

OWNER EDUCATION

"Behind every well-trained dog is a well-educated owner."

—Amy Pishner

Good puppy training starts with you! I am your coach, but ultimately *you* are your puppy's trainer. That is why I am devoting an entire chapter to owner education. You do not need a PhD in canine behavior to train your dog, but you *do* need to understand basic concepts in dog psychology and dog training.

That is what this chapter is all about. I start by teaching you how dogs learn, then I take a deep dive into this core tenet of my training philosophy. I teach you what you need to know about communication, motivation, and relationship as they relate to puppy training.

Are you excited to train your puppy?

If you embrace the information in this chapter, you will be *thinking* like a dog trainer in no time!

HOW DOGS LEARN

How much do you know about canine behavior and training? Do you know *how* dogs actually learn? Do not worry because I am not going to inundate you with confusing technical terms in the pages to come. I am going to teach you exactly what you need to know to get the wheels turning and head off in the right direction.

Let's start by reviewing some basic terms and definitions!

CLASSICAL CONDITIONING

Chances are, you have heard of Ivan Pavlov. He was a Russian psychologist who won a Nobel Prize for his classical conditioning experiments with dogs.

In the course of his research, Pavlov learned that dogs salivate prior to being fed. He began to ring a bell before feeding dogs and, over time, they began to salivate when they heard the bell.

Cha-ching!

The salivation was a conditioned reflex of unconscious learning. The development of such reflexes is called *classical conditioning*, also known as *Pavlovian conditioning*.

Conditioning is a powerful tool in dog training. It is intertwined in everything we do—from caring for our dogs to training them and socializing them. Conditioning parallels and dramatically impacts our training progress.

It is *that* powerful.

POSITIVE VS. NEGATIVE CONDITIONING

Conditioning can be positive and negative. The goal is to use conditioning to our advantage in dog training.

Positive conditioning is when dogs create positive associations with everyday life experiences. For example, let's say a puppy meets a ~~young,~~ kind child for the first time. The child pets the puppy gently and gives them treats. The puppy walks away from the experience with their head held high and, the next time a kid comes around, the puppy wants to go over and say hi.

Positive conditioning just took place.

Negative conditioning is when dogs associate something new or novel with something bad or negative. For example, a puppy goes to a dog park to socialize with other dogs. Let's say she is the smallest and youngest dog in the park and is repeatedly chased and trampled by the other dogs. She is shaking and trembling when she leaves the dog park and, the next time she sees dogs, she avoids them.

Negative conditioning took place.

Do you see the difference? In puppy raising, every experience matters. This is why I focus so much on setting puppies up for success every step of the way in my Puppy Head Start program.

(It is also one of the many reasons why I am not a fan of dog parks!)

OPERANT CONDITIONING

Operant conditioning, also called "instrumental conditioning," is attributed to B. F. Skinner, a Harvard professor. *Operant conditioning* asserts that the strength of a behavior is modified by reinforcement (rewards) and punishment (corrections).

Operant conditioning is the foundation upon which balanced training is built and is the core of everything we do in dog training. It is how we shape behavior and mold our dog's behavior into what we like.

Your dog is always learning. They are learning what you like (based on what you reward) and what you do not like (based on what you correct). What is allowed and what is not.

You need to be on your A game because your dog is watching and learning from you, your family, and any other pets in your pack.

Dogs are smart and they learn quickly!

In hands-on application, operant conditioning requires good timing. Reward what you like *right away* and correct what you do not like *right away.*

COUNTERCONDITIONING

This program is designed for puppies who are confident overall and have a clean slate. If you have an older puppy, a nervous puppy, or a puppy who has already had bad experiences, counterconditioning is going to come into play for you.

Counterconditioning is a technique used to help dogs overcome their fear by replacing negative responses to stimuli with positive ones. It involves pairing every presentation of a negative stimulus with something positive like food and play.

Counterconditioning is usually done in correlation with desensitization.

DESENSITIZATION

Desensitization is a process by which dogs are repeatedly exposed to a trigger at a very low intensity level and in a manner that is not overwhelming and does not create a fear response. Desensitization requires breaking problems down and approaching situations slowly and systematically. Doing so helps to keep the dog "at or under threshold," which means the dog is okay in their environment, not overly nervous, and is not shutting down or reacting poorly to the situation at hand.

Counterconditioning and desensitization both help to rewire the dog's brain and change the way they think. They are powerful tools in dog training! Both of these topics are covered in Chapter 14 (Problems and Solutions).

Now, let's talk about rewards and corrections.

THE FOUR QUADRANTS

There are four quadrants in dog training: positive reinforcement, negative reinforcement, positive punishment, and negative punishment.

1. *Positive reinforcement* (R+) means you reward your dog for good behavior.
2. For example, your puppy sits on command so you give them a treat.

3. *Negative reinforcement* (R-) means you stop correcting your dog when bad behavior stops.
4. For example, your puppy stops barking so you relax the slip lead and release the pressure.
5. *Positive punishment* (P+) means you correct your dog for bad behavior to make it stop.
6. For example, your puppy bites your hand so you pop them on the nose.
7. *Negative punishment* (P-) means you stop rewarding your dog when bad behavior starts.
8. For example, you stop petting your puppy when they start biting your hand.

WHAT TO DO AND WHEN

Do not worry about which quadrant to use in which specific situations. What is important is that you *embrace* all four quadrants. While I do use primarily positive reinforcement (rewards) in my foundation training, I also use the other three quadrants as needed.

Bottom line: I train the dog in front of me.

Your puppy is not going to be afraid of you for correcting them. It is actually quite the opposite. Your puppy will respect you and appreciate your transparency. They will see that you are not a doormat and are the pack leader.

Dogs learn best when training is simple and communication is clear. They live in a black-and-white world. Corrections bring clarity.

In my training, I pair science with common sense. It is a thing of beauty!

CMR

At the core of my training philosophy is something I have dubbed "CMR." *CMR* stands for "communication, motivation, and relationship." Over the years, I have discovered that good dog training embraces CMR and bad dog training ignores it.

Every single problem in dog training can be traced back to CMR. Every problem stems from a communication problem, a motivation problem, or a relationship problem.

Failed CMR is where problems start. Successful CMR is where solutions are found.

As your coach, I am going to teach you how to embrace CMR so you can embrace a fulfilling life with your puppy. After all, as Einstein once said, "*An ounce of prevention is worth a pound of cure.*"

CMR: COMMUNICATION

KISS ("keep it simple, stupid") is an old Navy principle. It means that most systems work best if they are simple as opposed to being complex. Simplicity is the goal with puppy training too!

Simple is good. Less is more.

Let me teach you how to keep communication simple, clean, and effective.

Amy and Havok, circa 2016. Photo credit: John Fisher Photography.

MARKER WORDS

First things first—do not talk your dog's ear off! Use only words that are meaningful to them. These include your dog's name, basic commands as you teach them, and marker words.

Marker words are words or sounds used to communicate to your dog that they are doing something correctly or incorrectly. Marker words mark a specific moment in time when your dog performs an action or behavior, streamlining the training process. They are feedback in its simplest form.

We use classical conditioning to teach marker words. We say the marker, pause for about a second, and then follow through with a reward or correction. Over time, the marker becomes a conditioned (and powerful) word.

In my training, I use three marker words: "good," "no," and "free."

1. **"Good"** is a reward marker. It means "That was correct. You are doing a good job. Keep doing what you are doing." The "Good" marker is followed by a reward (abbreviated R+). Initially, the reward is food. Later, the reward can be food, praise, or affection (whichever is best for the situation).
2. "**No"** is a correction marker. It means "That is not what I want. That is not what I asked for. Stop doing that." The "no" marker is followed by a correction, a redirection, or restating the command.
3. "**Free"** is a release marker. It means "You are released from the command. Come to me for a reward." We teach this marker by saying "Free," then stepping back and rewarding the dog. Initially, the reward is food. Later, it can be food, praise, or affection.

A FEW WORDS ON MARKERS

Markers should be said the same way, each time, without emotion. Emotion makes things foggy and makes the dog feel they must interpret the marker.

To use markers in training, they must first be taught to the dog. Do this by using classical conditioning: ("Good" + reward (food); "No" + correction; "Free" + step back and reward).

After marking, wait one second before following through with the reward (or correction).

The biggest mistake I see in marker training is referred to as "layering." Layering is when the marker and the reward (or correction) are given at the same time. Classical conditioning requires one thing to happen before the next, not both at the same time.

Ideally, you want to:

Mark the behavior + pause + follow through

Repetition is the key to successful conditioning. It takes anywhere from 120 to 150 quality repetitions for something to become conditioned in a dog's mind. Once dogs understand markers, better communication is established for the duration of training.

TONE OF VOICE

Tone of voice is the way you speak to someone (or in this case, your dog). In essence, it is how you sound when you say words out loud. In dog training, tone of voice matters a lot. It directly affects the outcome of your commands.

For example, if you ask your dog to sit like "Sit?," your dog hears that command as a request. They know there's the option to obey or not obey. If you had said "Sit," full stop, or "Sit!," your dog would have put their butt on the ground.

See what I mean?

I want you to use tone of voice to your advantage. For example, when I am teaching recall (the "Come" command) to my dog, I use a high-pitched, happy tone of voice with good inflection. I want my dog to *want* to come when called and am conditioning a positive response to my command.

The same goes for saying "No." I do not say "No" casually, and I certainly do not say it often. It is reserved for situations when I know my dog knows better. I say it loudly and firmly and look straight at my dog when I say it. After that is established, I follow through and stop my dog from doing the unwanted behavior.

No means no! Not yes. Not maybe.

Tone of voice, in my opinion, is one of the most underrated tools in dog training. It has the power to enhance your dog's obedience in ways that nothing else can and gets you in sync with your dog in a supernatural way.

NONVERBAL COMMUNICATION

Another way you can enhance communication with your dog is through the use of nonverbals. If I am being honest, we as a human race are terrible at reading body language. During my time in the military, I learned to read between the lines by watching body language and studying people.

It is a great skill to have and guess who else has it—your dog.

Dogs are body language experts, so stop talking to your dog and start paying attention to what your gestures, facial expressions, posture, and eye contact are saying to them.

This is the language your dog understands best! The question is, is your nonverbal body language communicating the same things that your words are saying? Furthermore, does it match your intentions?

Do not overwhelm yourself! You are not expected to master all of this in a day. But as you get into the swing of things, start challenging yourself to pay better attention to your body language during your training sessions.

Is your body language soft and relaxed, or do you appear angry or otherwise unhappy?

Videotaping your training sessions is a great way to hone in on your body language. Aim for soft body language during your training sessions and appropriate body language for everything else (when rewarding, be happy; when correcting, be stern).

When you do, your training will soar to new heights!

TIMING

Timing is a critical factor of communication in dog training. It is the essence of learning through association, which is how dogs learn. Research has shown that if you react to something your dog does within 0.5 to 2.3 seconds, or about a second, your dog is best able to learn.

If your dog does something you *do* like, you should reward them right away. If your dog does something you do *not* like, you should correct them right away. This helps your dog understand very clearly what is considered good and bad behavior.

Marker words help you have good timing. The better your timing, the more quickly your dog is able to learn.

STRUCTURE

Life is not and should not be a free-for-all for your puppy. Your puppy needs structure.

Structure is a pattern of organization and allows your puppy to coexist peacefully in your pack with certain physical limitations in place. It keeps your puppy in check and under control with little effort on your part.

What kind of structure should puppies have? There are three options:

Option One: Tethering

Tethering means connecting your puppy to you via a slip lead. Any time your puppy is out of the crate, they need to be tethered to you. They do not need unrestricted access to your house.

Tethering allows you to establish boundaries, rules, and expectations for your puppy and allows you to give instant feedback to your puppy regarding behaviors you like and behaviors you do not like.

If you want to be successful on your puppy training journey, you need to tether yourself to puppy while you are in the house. When you are outside, you can use a long line. In both situations, you need to have physical control.

As your puppy gets older, based on their behavior, off-leash freedom can be earned. You can start by dropping the slip lead or long line to see if your puppy makes good choices. Eventually, you can eliminate both as your puppy matures.

Do not give your puppy too much freedom too soon. You will end up *reacting* to your puppy's unwanted behavior instead of *preventing* it from happening in the first place.

Option Two: Crating

The crate is a godsend for dog training. Dogs are den-like animals. They like to be in a small, confined place to rest because it makes them feel safe. They do not have to worry about what is going on around them.

Later in this book, I will explain how to properly introduce your puppy to the crate. By doing so, your puppy will create a positive association with the crate and will love to be in it.

Crate training prevents problem behaviors, property destruction, and separation anxiety. It also helps with potty training. On average, puppies sleep eighteen hours a day, so letting your puppy take naps in the crate is a win-win for you and for your puppy!

Any time you are not actively supervising or training your puppy, put them in the crate. The crate provides structure in your absence. During the day, your puppy will likely nap for anywhere from one to three hours at a time before needing to get up and go potty outside.

Option Three: The Place Bed

The third and final structure option is the place bed. The place bed is a raised bed with defined edges. Dogs can stand up, sit, or lay on the bed. They cannot jump from it, bark from it, or get off of it.

The place bed allows your puppy to be in the room with you without getting underfoot. It is great for times when you are cooking, cleaning, or having friends over. The place bed calms your puppy down in the house and helps them habituate to everyday life.

I will teach you how to properly introduce and use the place bed in Chapter 8 (Obedience Training). Please do not use it before then.

CONSISTENCY

I saved the best for last! Of all the things in dog training, this is usually the toughest for dog owners and, consequently, it is one of the key factors to success in training.

Consistency means following through. Giving commands and upholding them. Establishing house rules and sticking to them. Teaching your dog to do something and then expecting them to do it every time.

If you live alone, consistency is easy. You are the only person responsible for your dog's behavior.

Consistency is harder for larger households with lots of family members, pets, moving parts, and pieces. When life gets busy, sometimes the first thing that goes out the window is consistency! Am I right?

But keep in mind, your puppy is counting on you. No excuses! Decide what is important. Do not be afraid to delegate. Be a good steward of your time.

Consistency may be hard, but it is worth it. Do your absolute best to be consistent with your puppy.

CMR: MOTIVATION

Motivation is such an important part of dog training because it is how you get your dog to do what you want and stop doing what you do not want. It is how you teach your dog new things and hold them accountable for her behavior.

Good dog training makes good use of motivators. Everything you use to motivate your dog is ammunition in your training arsenal, so stock up!

Let's start with rewards.

PRIMARY AND SECONDARY REINFORCERS

Primary reinforcers are reinforcers your dog needs for survival. There are four primary reinforcers: food, air, water, and sex. Dogs are hardwired to work for them! When you give your dog a piece of food in training, you are using a primary reinforcer. Toys, in many cases, are also primary reinforcers, because, in the dog's mind, the toy is prey and prey is food.

Secondary reinforcers, also called *conditioned reinforcers*, are things we condition dogs to like, such as praise, petting, smiling, eye contact, the clicker, and marker words. Secondary reinforcers gain value by being paired with primary reinforcers. For example, when you pet your dog while giving them a piece of food, you are conditioning your dog to see petting as a reward.

In layman's terms, I want you to think of reinforcers as rewards.

CORRECTIONS

In puppy training, we have a handful of corrections at our disposal, including pressure from the slip lead, withholding a food reward, and using our body to block or stop bad behavior. As our dog advances in training, we use a training collar to correct our dog for unwanted behavior. A training collar, such as a prong collar or an e-collar, should not be used with young puppies under six months of age. It is saved for later on in training when you are ready to proof your dog's training to distractions and finish their obedience. In early puppy training, a slip lead is all you need.

Your dog is going to learn very quickly which behaviors produce rewards and which behaviors produce corrections. In doing so, they will become motivated to avoid corrections from you and will avoid doing those associated behaviors.

This is a form of motivation!

If your boss withholds your pay for being late to work, you will start showing up on time. Right?

If you are consistently late, you will get fired.

My goal in dog training is to create a *thinking dog* who understands that actions have consequences. I do not want my dog to avoid me for fear of being corrected. I want them to understand which actions produce corrections and to refrain from doing those particular behaviors.

There is a big difference between fear and accountability.

BUILDING DRIVE

This is one of my favorite topics in dog training. Many dog owners think their dogs are not motivated by food, toys, praise, or affection.

They are wrong. All dogs are motivated!

What people fail to realize is that *drive is dynamic*. It is ever-changing based on lifestyle and circumstances.

Let's talk about food drive first. Dogs need food to survive, which means they are hardwired to work for food as a primary reinforcer. That is why we use food as a reward in training.

Most dogs love food and will work for it, but if your dog is a little bit picky, you will need to build their drive for food. You can do this by withholding food for twelve to twenty-four hours. (Yes, no food! Your dog will not die!) Exercise your dog an extra amount during that time and make sure they are given plenty of water to drink, but nothing to eat. After twelve hours, offer your dog a piece of food to see if they are hungry. If so, you can begin training. If not yet, wait another twelve hours. (Make sure your dog is being fed a quality kibble. Dogs know good food when they *smell* it!)

Every dog I have ever trained has shown good food drive after fasting. If your dog is not hungry after twenty-four hours of not eating, consult your veterinarian; your dog may not be feeling well.

Building food drive is easy. Deprivation builds motivation. The same goes for other reinforcers like praise, play, and affection. As your dog's owner, I want you to *play hard to get.* Make your dog earn praise, play, and affection. Do not give it out for free! Pair it with a primary reinforcer and make rewards fun.

The more your dog has to work to earn food, praise, play, affection, and other reinforcers, the more valuable those things will become. Building drive and motivation is all about increasing the inherent value of the reinforcers you are using.

It is easy if you use common sense.

PREMACKING

The *Premack principle* states that high-probability behavior reinforces low-probability behavior. What does this mean? It means that if your dog wants something, or wants *to do something*, wait for them to offer the behavior *you* want before giving the reward *they* want.

Your dog wants to go outside? Great. First, they need to offer a sit at the door. Then the door will open. Your dog wants to be petted? First, they need to sit, and then you can pet them. Simple!

Premacking is a powerful concept. Many breeders employ it for several weeks before their puppies leave their homes. They teach puppies to sit nicely for attention, to not jump on people, to wait for their food, and to wait to go outside. It is awesome! I love breeders who proactively train *thinking* puppies who can problem-solve and think outside the box.

JACKPOTTING

Jackpotting involves rewarding a dog heavily for performing the correct desired behavior for the first time. Jackpotting strengthens behavior and is reserved for "*Aha!*" moments in dog training when things just…*click!*

For example, if you are teaching "Shake" and your puppy offers you their paw for the first time, *jackpot!* Throw a little party! Give your puppy lots of food, praise, and affection. Clap! Show how pleased you are with what they just did.

After celebrating for twenty to thirty seconds or so, end the session. This is the best way to end on a good note, which is always the goal in dog training.

Jackpotting should be used rarely, not every day and definitely not every session. It highlights exceptional behavior and is used to communicate a job well done.

CMR: RELATIONSHIP

When it comes to your relationship with your dog, I want to help you start off on the right foot. Your dog knows you, and they have already created an idea of who you are, what you are like, and what kind of leader you are. If you have done a good job as your dog's leader, then you likely have a good relationship with your dog. If you have not done a good job as your dog's leader, then it is time to make some changes.

Having a healthy relationship with your dog is a key aspect to successful dog training. Your new and improved relationship with your dog starts today.

Let me help you!

CALM AND ASSERTIVE IS THE GOAL

Starting today, your goal is to be a calm and assertive leader for your dog.

Calm, assertive leaders are self-assured, not excited, confident but not aggressive, and not agitated. They maintain their composure and do not lose their temper. A calm, assertive leader has good *emotional intelligence*, which is the ability to perceive, interpret, evaluate, and control one's own emotions.

Are you calm and assertive? If not, that should be your goal.

Never train when you are tired, hungry, or upset. If you grow frustrated with your dog, stop what you are doing, put your dog in the crate, and take a break. Losing your temper will hurt the relationship you are building with your dog.

No training is better than bad training. Remember that your energy goes straight down the leash to your puppy.

THE 10/10 RULE

On a scale of one to ten (with one being low and ten being high), how much leadership do you provide your dog? On that same scale, how would you rate yourself in terms of affection with your dog?

On average, most dog owners admit to being somewhere between two and four in leadership and eight to ten in affection.

There is a problem there. Too much affection without leadership is a recipe for disaster!

All too often, we love to love our dogs, and we fail to lead them.

Your goal as a dog owner is to find balance. If you are a three in leadership and a nine in affection, then you need to bump up your leadership and cut back on affection.

As a dog trainer, I am a ten out of ten. I am big on affection when the time is right and big on leadership. My dogs know what is expected of them and look to me for guidance and information.

My goal as a professional dog trainer is to make sure my dog owners become great leaders for their dogs.

TRUST AND RESPECT

Trust and respect are like an old married couple. They go hand in hand. Your goal in dog training is to foster a healthy relationship with your dog—a relationship that is based on trust and respect.

How do you build trust with your dog? Through physical exercise, mental stimulation, confidence building, and training. Trust is not just about fairness. You have to be *firm but fair* to gain your dog's trust. You have to be a good leader! Being soft is seen as weakness. Dogs flee from weak owners and cling to strong owners because they are pack animals rooted in survival.

If you want your dog's trust, you need to demand their respect. You can do this by establishing boundaries, rules, and expectations, and by holding your dog accountable for their behavior. When I tell you, metaphorically, to put your foot down, *I mean it*!

ANTHROPOMORPHISM

Your dog is not a "fur baby" or a child; they are a dog. D. O. G.

Anthropomorphism is attributing human motivation, characteristics, or behavior to inanimate objects, animals, or natural phenomena. It is as silly as saying that plants get mad when you go away on vacation. Crazy, right?

Your computer is not mad at you. The wind does not talk. Dogs are not people. Stop anthropomorphizing!

If you want to be a successful dog owner, you need to treat your dog *like a dog*. You can love them deeply, but you need to realize that, no matter how much you love them, at the end of the day, your dog is a dog.

A canine. *Canis*. Descendant of the *Canis lupus*.

As such, they deserve a strong pack leader who does not spoil them, does not try to be their friend, and does not treat them like a human child.

CONFIDENCE BUILDING

We are going to cover a lot of confidence building in this program. Every time you work with your puppy, introduce something new, and go on a field trip, you are building their confidence. There is no such thing as too much confidence building!

Every dog can benefit from it—even genetically bombproof dogs! Confidence building teaches dogs how to handle and overcome stress and be resilient.

Do you want to know the best part? The more confidence building you do with your puppy, the better your relationship is going to be. Confidence building cements a strong bond with your dog and teaches you to work together as a team.

The world is full of confidence-building opportunities, which we will explore in this book. I will show you exactly how to build your dog's confidence!

THE LITTLE STUFF

The little stuff matters too, by the way. What do I mean? I mean that if you give your dog an inch, they will take a mile. If you make a rule and then you bend it, you are setting them up to fail.

If you let your dog jump on you when they were a puppy and now get mad at them for jumping on you because they are big, who is at fault? You are.

Pay attention to the little stuff because, over time, it leads to big problems. If there is something you want your puppy to do, or not do, then you need to have a clear image in your head of what that looks like. What is allowed and what is not? The little stuff matters.

I am very picky about *the little stuff* with puppies in training. I have my reasons because I know that if I allow puppies to do something, like biting the leash or jumping on me, then I am failing them.

If you nip a problem in the bud, you stop it from growing.

The Big Three

Dogs need three things to be satisfied. I call them *The Big Three*: physical exercise, mental stimulation, and training. Physical exercise tires your dog out physically. Mental stimulation tires your dog out mentally. Training provides the framework upon which your dog's lifestyle and behaviors are built.

In this book, I teach you how to meet your puppy's needs for The Big Three in ways that are meaningful, safe, and age-appropriate. Responsible, loving dog owners recognize their dog's needs and fulfill them on a regular basis.

Chapter Summary

Communication, motivation, and relationship (CMR) are the three pillars of dog training. When you understand your role in each one and how to best help your dog, you will see that training a dog is a bit easier than you thought! Consistency is key. Just by reading this chapter, you have a jumpstart on being a great dog owner.

You can do it!

4.

THE FIRST FORTY-EIGHT HOURS

"The beginning is the most important part of the work."
—Plato

Bringing your new puppy home is fun and exciting, and there is a lot of anticipation surrounding your new puppy's arrival. In this chapter, I teach you how to have an enjoyable and stress-free first forty-eight hours.

I start with packing lists for local and long-distance pick-ups, then guide you through the process of getting your puppy home. I have even included a list of *dos* and *don'ts* for you to use at home. Some of these will help when you introduce the crate, establish a potty schedule, and start training!

Read this chapter before picking up your puppy. If you already have your puppy, feel free to skim this chapter and look for things you have done correctly or incorrectly so far.

You will be glad you did!

PICKING UP YOUR PUPPY

LOCAL PICK-UPS

If you are picking up your puppy locally, bring the following items:

- your puppy's crate
- a hand towel for inside the crate
- a lightweight blanket or towel to cover the crate with
- poop bags
- a slip lead

LONG-DISTANCE PICK-UPS

If you are traveling a long distance to pick up your puppy, your packing list is more involved.

Bring the following:

- your puppy's crate
- two or three small towels for inside the crate
- a lightweight blanket or towel to cover the crate with
- poop bags
- a slip lead
- paper towels
- multipurpose cleaning spray
- puppy wipes
- a trash bag
- food for the puppy
- water for the puppy
- food and water bowls
- Vibactra Immune Support bottle
- Kochi Free Healthy Stools bottle
- doggie shampoo
- bath towel

For long-distance pick-ups, it is best for your puppy to ride in the crate. Put them in the crate and cover it before the journey home. When your puppy wakes up in the crate, they will probably need to potty. Find a non-pet populated area, pull over, put the slip lead on, and walk them for a few minutes.

When you give your puppy food and water, make sure you only give them a little bit at a time. You do not want them to get sick or throw up in the car. If you are stopping overnight at a hotel, cut off food and water *three hours* before bedtime.

Overnight, your puppy will need to be let out every three to four hours. I usually potty puppies at midnight, then again around four in the morning.

If your puppy is staying in your car overnight, make sure you keep an eye on the weather. Once the sun comes out, it can heat up quickly in a vehicle.

For best results, exercise your puppy before loading them into the crate. A tired puppy is a good puppy. Ultimately, though, your puppy is probably going to cry in the crate. It is perfectly fine and normal.

Frequent potty breaks are the key to success for long car rides. If your puppy has an accident in the crate, clean them and the crate as soon as possible.

Give your puppy Vibactra and Kochi Free tinctures at mealtimes to boost their immune system and help prevent diarrhea. Do this for the first few weeks until the bottles are empty.

AIRPORT PICK-UPS

If you are picking your puppy up from any airport, DO NOT take them out of the crate at the airport and DO NOT use the pet relief station inside or outside the airport. Load your puppy (still in their crate) directly into your vehicle, drive at least thirty minutes to a pet-safe area, and then let your puppy out so they can stretch their legs. After your puppy potties, clean them up, give them some food and water, and then put them back in the crate.

THIS IS VERY IMPORTANT—the pet relief areas outside of airports are almost certainly contaminated with parvo and other transferable diseases from pets frequenting them from around the world. You do not want to expose your puppy to global diseases, so this is why it is important to keep your puppy safely tucked away in the crate until you leave the airport and take them someplace else.

DRIVING ALONE

If you are driving alone, put the crate in the back of your vehicle. Once you have possession of your puppy, give them some cuddles and then put them directly into the crate and cover it. Do not attempt to drive home with a puppy in your lap. This is not only distracting but it can also be dangerous. If your puppy whines and cries in the crate, do not worry about it. Just focus on getting home in one piece.

DRIVING WITH SOMEONE ELSE

If someone else is driving, you can put your puppy in your lap if you would like. I like to use a small towel to help cushion my puppy and make my lap more comfortable. Encourage your puppy to stay in one place by placing your hand over your puppy's body and petting it slowly and gently from head to rump. If you are excited, your puppy will be too. You want to comfort your puppy without amping them up.

If you do not wish to keep your puppy on your lap, put them in the crate.

To prevent car sickness, do not give your puppy food or water before the ride home.

If your puppy wakes up in the crate or starts to get squirmy in your lap, they probably need to go potty. Find a spot off the beaten path to pull over. Avoid parks, pet stores, and other pet-populated areas.

To be safe, you can put the slip lead on your puppy for the potty break if you want to. Simply slide the slip lead over their head and slide the tab down to secure it in place. Keep the leash loose and walk your puppy around for a minute or two. If they go potty, great! If not, load them back into the car.

AT HOME WITH YOUR PUPPY

Once you arrive home, the fun begins! This is when you get to really enjoy your puppy. You begin to learn more about their personality, and you get to start raising and training them. It is an important period of time. There are things you *should* do and things you *should not do* during the first forty-eight hours.

THE TEN DOS:

1. TAKE YOUR PUPPY ON A POTTY WALK.

A tired puppy is a good puppy. You are going to hear me say this a lot because it is true! When you first get home with your puppy, give them a few sips of water, then take them for a walk. A ten to fifteen-minute walk should suffice because it will allow your puppy to expel some energy and go potty if they need to. If your puppy is especially rambunctious, a longer walk might be necessary!

If you have other dogs, do NOT take them along. Other (human) family members are welcome.

Try to not step on your puppy. Eight-week-old puppies are very clingy and surprisingly good at getting under your feet. If you shuffle your feet as you slowly walk, you should be able to avoid stepping on your puppy. Try to ignore them rather than giving them attention if they jump on you. Keep walking. (I recommend wearing pants so your legs do not get scratched!)

I call these short walks "*potty walks.*" They are an important part of your puppy's potty training and overall mental health. If you have property or a large fenced area, you can do potty walks off leash. If you have a small fenced yard, you can walk laps around your yard and your puppy should follow you. At eight weeks of age, puppies usually stay pretty close, so do not worry about your puppy running off. If your puppy is older or if you do not feel comfortable letting them off leash, use your harness and long line to make walks secure.

At this age, for safety reasons, never take your puppy to unknown areas or places where other dogs might be.

2. GIVE YOUR PUPPY A LONG DRINK OF WATER.

After your walk, allow them to drink some water to make sure they are well hydrated and feeling good. After twenty to thirty minutes have passed, take them on another potty walk.

3. HAVE YOUR PUPPY START WORKING FOR FOOD.

Training already, you ask? Yes! You will start training on day one. This jumpstarts the bonding process and provides puppies with mental stimulation so they are tired before going into the crate. Sessions are short and sweet (two to three minutes max). Use food as your primary reward.

4. FEED KIBBLE WITH VIBACTRA AND KOCHI FREE.

Use the food your puppy is used to first, if possible, then slowly transition your puppy over the course of two to three weeks to your kibble of choice. Give Vibactra and the Kochi Free with food for immune support and to help ward off diarrhea. You can feel free to squirt the tincture directly into the back of your puppy's mouth or drop it over some food in a bowl.

If your puppy has diarrhea, refer to Chapter 14 (Problems and Solutions) and look up "Diarrhea."

5. POTTY YOUR PUPPY FREQUENTLY.

Young puppies have small bladders and need to potty often. Your puppy's potty schedule is time-based and needs-based. Let me explain.

Time-based means your puppy needs to go potty thirty minutes after drinking water, two hours after eating food, every two to three hours throughout the day, and every three to four hours at night (for the first few weeks or so).

Needs-based means your puppy needs to go potty after waking up from a nap, before training, after training, before playtime, after playtime, and any time they act squirmy or restless, or start whining, pacing, sniffing, or walking around in a circle.

When in doubt, potty your puppy! It is going to feel like *a lot,* but trust me, it is necessary. Pottying your puppy takes two minutes. Cleaning a dirty crate and a dirty puppy takes twenty to thirty minutes. You tell me which one is easier!

When pottying your puppy, carry them outside to the spot where you want them to go potty, then put them down, ignore them, and walk around a little (back and forth, side to side). Wait for your puppy to go potty, then praise them. If they need to go potty, they should go within sixty seconds (max). If they do not go, take them back inside, hold onto them for a few minutes, and then try again.

When they are done pottying, carry them back inside. Potty time is NOT combined with playtime in any way, shape, or form. It is a distinct and isolated event. Do not bring kibble with you for potty breaks. It can be distracting for highly food-motivated puppies who want the food and do not realize you want them to go potty instead.

6. INTRODUCE YOUR PUPPY TO OTHER HOUSEHOLD FAMILY MEMBERS.

It is perfectly okay to introduce your puppy to other household family members right away; just ask them to be calm. They can pick your puppy up, as long as they can be trusted not to drop them. Your puppy can even stay on the floor for the meet and greet if you prefer. If your puppy is on the floor, place your hands on their chest and shoulders to keep them from jumping up if they get excited. Do not allow your puppy to jump, bite, or scratch anyone.

Introductions are best done when puppies are tired, at the end of the day or after potty walks.

7. GIVE FOOD AND WATER ON A SCHEDULE.

Your puppy should receive the majority of their allotted food and water in the first half of the day. This gives you plenty of time to potty them as much as needed before bedtime.

Do several short training sessions—using a food reward—so that your puppy is earning their kibble, and remember to give them a little water after training because they will be thirsty!

Do not give your puppy unlimited access to food and water or large amounts of food and water at once. This can lead to diarrhea and accidents in the crate.

8. WAIT UNTIL YOUR PUPPY IS TIRED BEFORE PUTTING THEM IN THE CRATE.

Tired is good! If you are lucky, your puppy's breeder or rescue has already introduced crate training so your puppy associates the crate with sleep. That is what you want!

Many puppies are not so fortunate. Some have never been in a crate before, and others *have* been in a crate but do not like it. Most puppies throw a fit when they are put in the crate, so this is why exercising your puppy ahead of time and tiring them out is so important.

9. USE THE CRATE.

Crate and rotate—that is the name of the game! Any time your puppy is out of the crate, you should be supervising them. Any time you can't, they need to go back in the crate. Plain and simple.

When putting your puppy in the crate, follow this protocol:

1. Carry your puppy into the crate room.
2. Open the crate door.
3. Put your puppy in.
4. Close the crate door.
5. Cover the crate with a towel or blanket.
6. Turn on a fan or other white noise.

7. Turn off the light.
8. Leave the room and close the door.

Keep noise to a minimum outside the crate room door. Ignore your puppy if and when they cry. Some puppies scream like banshees. Others cry only a little before quieting down.

Do not—I repeat, DO NOT—take your puppy out of the crate when they are screaming. Let them cry it out. They are perfectly fine. Once they settle down, they should take a nap. If they settle down but do not nap, you can go in and take them out as a reward for being quiet.

When taking your puppy out of the crate, do this:

1. Go into the crate room calmly.
2. Open the crate door without saying a word.
3. Take your puppy out.
4. Turn off the fan or white noise.
5. Carry them outside to go potty.

No drama. No coddling. No fanfare.

It is very important that you *only* take your puppy out of the crate when they are quiet. You are conditioning their behavior and teaching them that calm behavior gets them out. Period.

10. TIRE YOUR PUPPY OUT BEFORE BED.

Before bedtime, it is important to tire puppies out so they sleep well overnight. When it is dark out, it is not ideal to take your puppy on a potty walk because there is too much out there that could startle them and cause them to run off. It's difficult to supervise your puppy in the dark.

For these reasons, I like to use a small toy to play with my puppy on a non-slip surface like a rug or carpet. Never play with young puppies on slick floors because it can hurt their joints.

These sessions involve lots of back-and-forth tug play with some fetch thrown in if your puppy is up for it. Sessions are short and low key. The goal is to tire your puppy out, not amp them up.

Those are the ten dos. Now let's talk about what you *shouldn't* do.

THE FIVE DON'TS

1. DON'T LET YOUR PUPPY BITE YOU.

Training starts right away. You do not need to correct your puppy for biting just yet, but you do need to prevent them from biting in the first place.

Do not pet them when they are excited. Do not put them on the floor or run from them. Do not put your hands near their mouth. The way you hold them, the amount of exercise they get, and the energy you project will all affect how much they try to bite you. Young puppies can learn to respect calm, assertive energy.

Eight-week-old puppies are usually not very mouthy. This behavior generally starts around nine to ten weeks of age.

2. DON'T LET YOUR PUPPY OUT OF YOUR SIGHT.

Any time your puppy is out of the crate, you should be carrying them or watching them like a hawk. Never let them out of your sight. Freedom for a young puppy usually leads to problems like unwanted chewing, accidents in the house, and other naughty behaviors. Carry your puppy from room to room in the house, putting them down for only brief moments if need be. Keep them close by when outside.

The only exception is in the evening, before bedtime, and after a potty break. Put your puppy down on the floor in the crate room to play with them and tire them out.

3. DON'T INTRODUCE YOUR PUPPY TO OTHER PACK MEMBERS.

Do not introduce your puppy to other pets in the first two days. It is not necessary. There is too much excitement surrounding the newcomer's arrival, so it is best to wait for the novelty to wear off before doing introductions. This goes for dogs, cats, and any other animals you might have.

If you have other pets, it is best to have a friend watch them if possible or keep them in a separate section of the house until your puppy has time to settle in and get acquainted with their new home and family.

I teach you in Chapter 9 (Socialization and Exposure) how to properly introduce your new puppy to other animal pack members. There is a time and a place for everything, so please be patient with the process.

4. DON'T GROOM YOUR PUPPY UNLESS ABSOLUTELY NECESSARY.

Do not give your puppy a bath or trim their nails unless you have to. Grooming at this age causes undue stress, which can lead to diarrhea. Diarrhea is a beast to stop once it starts and throws a curveball into your potty-training efforts. Only bathe your puppy if you really need to.

5. DON'T GO ON FIELD TRIPS.

Do not take your puppy anywhere for the first forty-eight hours. This is also unnecessary. Socialization and exposure can wait. Give your puppy time to settle in. If people want to come over to see your puppy, that is fine, but, in all honesty, it is best if they do not. Your puppy has experienced enough change and excitement already. There is no need for more!

PREPARING FOR TRAINING

You will need a treat pouch for your puppy's first training session. Take a Ziploc bag and put one cup of kibble inside it. Then place the bag inside your treat pouch. This will be your puppy's food reward during your training session. The Ziploc bag keeps your treat pouch clean and free of food oils.

The proper way to hold and deliver a piece of food to your puppy is to place the kibble in your hand between your pointer and middle fingers at the first knuckle. Hold it in place with your thumb.

When you hand the food to your puppy, point your fingers to the ground and hold your hand out, slightly curved, until your puppy licks it. At that point, slide your thumb away and let your puppy have the piece of food. Give your puppy one piece of food at a time to keep from dropping food accidentally.

YOUR FIRST TRAINING SESSION

Your first training session is here! You are going to do several short sessions with your puppy over the next forty-eight hours. The goal is to introduce your puppy to a food reward and start teaching your puppy the skill of luring. If you have an older puppy, you will also introduce the slip lead.

By having your puppy start working for food, you are meeting your puppy's needs for mental stimulation and training. This is a much better approach than feeding your puppy from a bowl. By using a food reward, you are practicing existential feeding, which is a great way to begin bonding with your puppy and get training underway.

Check out my website for a free training video on how to introduce your puppy to luring and working for food: www.valork9academyonline.com.

To introduce luring, start by putting a piece of dog food in your right hand between your second and third finger at the first knuckle, held in place with your thumb. Bring your hand down to your puppy's level and show the piece of food to your puppy. Once your puppy begins to sniff the food, mark "Good" and reward your puppy with that piece of food by sliding your thumb off the piece of food.

Do this several times until your puppy learns that the piece of food is in your hand.

Once your puppy catches on to that, present the piece of food palm-up, and as your puppy begins to sniff it, take a small step back. When your puppy follows the food in your hand, mark "Good" and reward. Repeat this several times until you are able to do it with both hands, stepping back.

From there, begin luring your puppy is large circles in front of you. Keep your hand at your puppy's mouth level—not high and not low—so your puppy can learn to follow the food anywhere it goes. Mark "Good" and reward for partial and complete circles in both directions (clockwise and counterclockwise).

FIRST TRAINING SESSION REMINDERS

Begin training in a quiet room of your house that is free of distractions so your puppy's focus is on you and the food in your hand. You will have your puppy work for all their food by doing this simple luring exercise for the next two days. The bigger your puppy is, the more they will eat.

Please note that if your puppy is distracted, it can be helpful to turn on a fan or white noise in the room you are working in. This helps to drown out noise around you and allows your puppy to better focus on you.

Keep your sessions short (two or three minutes maximum). If your puppy does not appear to be interested in the food, it may be that they are not hungry. Try fasting them for twelve hours, then offer food again. The goal is to train *only* when your puppy is hungry and motivated.

A hungry puppy is a motivated puppy! If your puppy is not hungry after twelve hours or appears lethargic, call your veterinarian.

EXAMPLE SCHEDULE

By now you might be wondering, "*What should my puppy's daily schedule look like?*"

Here is an example of a good puppy schedule:

0400 Potty break, then back in crate
0800 Potty walk, then back in crate
1000 Potty break, training session, water, back in crate
1030 Potty break, training session, water, back in crate
1100 Potty break, training session, water, back in crate
1300 Potty walk, then back in crate
1500 Potty break, training session, water, back in crate
1530 Potty break, training session, water, back in crate
1700 Potty walk, water, then hanging out outside
1900 Potty break, then back in crate
2000 Potty break, play session, potty break, back in crate
2400 Potty break, then back in crate

You are going to be busy! Your puppy needs lots of potty breaks, a handful of training sessions, a few potty walks, and some downtime in the evening to hang out and play.

A little bit of this and a little bit of that—that is a good puppy schedule!

This schedule is similar to what you will use—give or take—in the weeks to come as you knock out more intensive training.

Chapter Summary

Your primary goals are to:

- prevent your puppy from having an accident in the crate
- begin figuring out your puppy's potty schedule
- tire your puppy out before putting them in the crate

If you are worried the above schedule includes too much crate time, do not be. Puppies sleep for eighteen hours a day or more. They need rest. It is essential for growth.

As you go about your day with a new puppy, you might feel like you are taking care of a newborn baby, and you are not wrong! As a mom, I can tell you there are certainly a lot of similarities.

Diaper change. Nurse. Play. Sleep. Repeat. All. Day. Long.

Puppy training is a marathon, not a sprint.

Trust the process, stay the course, and you will have a successful first forty-eight hours!

5.

POTTY TRAINING

"Consistent hard work leads to success. Greatness will come."

—Dwayne "The Rock" Johnson

Potty training, also called housebreaking or house-training, can be intimidating for puppy owners. Many people relate it to child potty training and assume that it will happen, in time, when the dog is ready. That could not be more untrue!

Puppies can and should start potty training on day one. And like I say, the goal is to work smarter not harder, especially when it comes to potty training!

After personally potty training hundreds of puppies, I have some tricks up my sleeve. I am going to share them with you in this chapter so you will be able to potty train your puppy in a matter of weeks, not months or years.

I have broken up potty training into three phases with milestones for each. Phase 1 is for puppies eight to twelve weeks of age, Phase 2 is for puppies twelve to sixteen weeks of age, and Phase 3 is for puppies sixteen weeks of age and older.

If your puppy is more than eight weeks old, start in Phase 1 anyway. Do not move up to Phase 2 unless your puppy has successfully accomplished all the milestones for Phase 1.

Let's begin!

PHASE 1: 8–12 WEEKS OF AGE

Phase 1 starts on day one when you bring your puppy home and start establishing a feeding and pottying schedule. It continues through the next four weeks or until your puppy is twelve weeks old. I am going to break down the major components of potty training so that you know what to do with your puppy.

USE THE CRATE

If you want to be successful with potty training, you absolutely need to use the dang crate! You will not have much success without it. Crate training and potty training go hand-in-hand. The crate provides structure in your absence and helps to prevent accidents in the house.

Dogs are den-like animals. They crave small spaces to sleep in because it makes them feel safe. Do not anthropomorphize your dog and assume they will feel claustrophobic in a crate. They may fight it at first but, in the end, the crate will be their safe space.

In Phase 1, you will put your puppy in the crate, close the crate door, cover the crate with a blanket or towel, turn the lights off, turn on white noise, exit the room, and shut the door behind you.

That is it and in that order.

No talking to your dog. No offering words of comfort. Put them in the crate and leave.

FIGURE OUT YOUR PUPPY'S SCHEDULE

Initially, you are going to potty your puppy on a time-based and needs-based schedule.

You will potty your puppy:

- thirty minutes after drinking
- two hours after eating
- every three to four hours at night
- every two to three hours throughout the day
- after waking up from a nap
- before training
- after training
- before playtime
- after playtime
- any time your puppy gets restless or squirmy, starts pacing and whining, or begins sniffing and walking around in a tight circle—that means they have to go!

If you are lucky, you will have a puppy who can sleep a little longer than three to four hours at night before needing to go potty. Some puppies can "hold it" for five to six hours right out the gate!

At night, do not wait for your puppy to cry before letting them out. The key is setting your alarm and pottying them *before* they need to go out. This teaches them to sleep through the night.

If your puppy has an accident in the crate at night, it means you did not get up soon enough to let them out, so adjust accordingly.

With most puppies, you will get up at the same time each night for the first two weeks. Then you will get up incrementally later for the next two weeks after that. This will help you ease into Phase 2, which has no potty breaks in the middle of the night.

During the day, if you are not able to let your puppy out yourself, you need to line up someone who can. It is unfair to expect a puppy to go more than three hours without a potty break. Perhaps a neighbor, friend, or dogsitter can let out your puppy for you or maybe you can bring your puppy to work.

PICK A POTTY SPOT

Where do you want your puppy to potty? If you have an immaculate lawn, you may have a certain area where you want your puppy to potty. That is great. Teach your puppy to potty there—and only there—by taking them to that spot every time.

POTTY TIME

When it is time to go outside to potty, *carry your puppy*. Do not allow them to walk out of the crate themselves and do not expect them to follow you all the way outside. If they need to go, they may end up going potty in the house.

Instead, carry them to the potty spot, set them down, ignore them, and walk around slowly in the potty area until they go potty. Keep a close eye on your puppy but do not stare directly at them. Ignore them if they jump on you.

When they start to go potty, do not say anything. It might cause them to get excited and "cut it off." Wait until they are 90 percent done, then say, "Good girl, go potty!" Over time, they will begin to associate "Go potty" with the action of going potty. This is how you begin teaching them to potty on command.

After the potty break, pick them up and carry them back inside. Do not give them treats or play with them outside after potty time. Potty breaks are succinct activities that should not be combined with anything else. We want our puppies to go potty right away, not lollygag around.

Important to note: When pottying your puppy, only give them about two minutes to do their business. If they do not potty in those two minutes, time is up! Try again in five to ten minutes.

You will thank me when it's wintertime and your puppy has learned to potty immediately, on command, when and where you want them to. Good potty habits start now!

ACCIDENTS HAPPEN

Not if, but when your puppy has an accident, how you handle it is very impactful.

Do not yell at your puppy or get mad.

If your puppy had an accident in the crate, in Phase 1, it is *your fault*—not your puppy's. An accident means your puppy had too much to eat, too much to drink, or you did not get there in time when they woke up and needed to go out.

When your puppy has an accident, take them out of the crate and bathe them right away. Wash the parts of their body that are soiled. For example, if only their feet and belly are soiled, wash only those. I call this a *mini bath*. Too much unnecessary bathing strips your puppy's skin of its natural oils and can lead to dry, itchy skin.

Clean your puppy well, dry them off, and give them to someone to hold (if possible) while you clean the crate. Use Dawn dish soap and clean the crate well—all the cracks and crevices! It needs to smell brand-new by the time you are done with it. If your puppy peed in the crate, the hand towel in it can probably be salvaged. If your puppy pooped, throw the towel away and replace it with a new one. It is not worth saving.

Once the crate is clean, potty your puppy again before putting them back in the crate.

POTTY WALKS

Like I said in the last chapter, I am a big fan of potty walks. I love taking my dogs for a walk on our property. We all get fresh air and exercise.

Take your puppy on potty walks wherever you can safely do so—your backyard, an empty lot nearby, a trail, or an open field. Be sure to avoid areas frequented by other dogs.

I try to take puppies on three to four potty walks each day. By twelve weeks of age, these walks are usually twenty minutes long.

Rain, sleet, or snow—go for a walk! Walking in different types of weather teaches your puppy to be unbothered by it.

OTHER DOGS

If you have other dogs, do not bring them along initially when you take your puppy outside to go potty. They will distract your puppy and could cause them to not go potty when they should.

SUPERVISION IS KEY

I have said this before, and I will say it again—supervision is key. When your puppy is in Phase 1, they should not have any unsupervised time (except structured alone time, which we will talk about in Chapter 9).

When your puppy is in the house, keep a leash on them. When your puppy is outside, keep a close eye on them or use your long line and harness.

If you leave your puppy to their own devices, they will find things to get into and may start having accidents in the house. Once your house starts to stink like pee and poop, you are on a slippery slope to failed potty training.

You want your puppy to potty where they *always* potty: OUTSIDE!

CLEANING UP

If your puppy has an accident in the house, clean it well with soap and use a one-to-one solution of white vinegar and water to remove the odor. Take the soiled paper towels and put them outside in the usual potty spot, let your puppy sniff them, and tell them to "Go potty." This is an old trick that works well because dogs are simple association creatures.

Do not rub your puppy's nose in the pee or poop or yell at your puppy for having accidents in the house. Doing this can create a puppy who is afraid to go potty in front of you, which can cause your potty-training efforts outside to backfire on you.

POTTY BELLS

I am not a fan of potty bells. When a dog rings the potty bell, it is their way of saying, "*I want to go outside.*" It does not necessarily mean, "*I need to go potty.*" For a lot of dogs, this is a way to go outside to explore and play rather than go potty.

Try to learn your puppy's potty routine and tell-tale signs of needing to go outside. Put your puppy on a potty schedule. They will be potty-trained in no time—without the use of a bell.

USE THE KOCHI FREE

Kochi Free is packed with herbs that will help to solidify your puppy's stool and prevent diarrhea. Give it to your puppy once a day for best results.

COPROPHAGIA

Coprophagia is a fancy word for "poop eater." If you catch your puppy eating poop, refer to Chapter 14 for help.

THE GOAL

The goal for Phase 1 is to be on a team that I made up—*Team No Accidents*. To be on *Team No Accidents,* your puppy must successfully potty outside every time and never have an accident in the house or crate. Do you think you can do it? It is a great goal to have.

MILESTONES

To move from Phase 1 to Phase 2, I want you to achieve the following milestones:

1. Your puppy is waiting to go outside instead of pottying in the crate.

2. Your puppy is pottying relatively quickly when you take them outside to go potty.
3. Your puppy has not had an accident in the crate at all or for at least two weeks.
4. You feel confident that you have a good food, water, exercise, and potty schedule figured out.

If you can answer "Yes" to all four, congratulations! You are ready to move to Phase 2. If you cannot answer "Yes" to all four, stay in Phase 1 until you are confident you are ready for Phase 2.

PHASE 2: 12–16 WEEKS OF AGE

In Phase 2, you're going to continue doing everything you were doing in Phase 1 but with a few modifications.

PHASE OUT LATE-NIGHT POTTY BREAKS

Your puppy is older and bigger now, so you can start phasing out those middle-of-the-night potty breaks. Do so gradually. Instead of letting them out at 4:00 a.m., for example, let them out at 5:00 a.m. and then the next day at 6:00 a.m. By spacing out potty breaks, you are helping them learn to "hold it" for longer periods of time overnight. If you are lucky, they will soon be sleeping through the night.

"HOLDING IT" FOUR TO SIX HOURS DURING THE DAY

As your puppy's bladder gets bigger, their naps should become longer, which means they can go longer between potty breaks. This makes your life much easier. You have more freedom to run errands or even work a longer shift without bringing your puppy to work with you or lining up someone to give them a potty break.

TRAIN FIRST, THEN POTTY

At this point, you should be able to take your puppy out of the crate and train them before taking them out to potty. This is a sign that your puppy is developing bladder control and no longs needs to potty immediately upon waking.

The only exception, of course, is if they are doing the "potty dance" and clearly need to go out. If they need to go potty, take them potty. If they seem comfortable, train first and potty later, after the training session is finished.

WALKING TO THE POTTY SPOT

Since your puppy's bladder is bigger now, you should be able to lead your puppy outside to the potty spot. If you are really lucky, you will be able to open the door, let your puppy out, watch them go potty on their own, and when they are done, watch them come back inside!

A three-month-old puppy taking themselves out to potty—it does not get better than that!

TELLING YOU WHEN THEY NEED TO GO OUT

"Clean" puppies do not want to mess in their crates. They let you know when they need to go potty. Usually, this starts in Phase 2, but sometimes it starts sooner. They wake up from their nap and offer a few high-pitched yips or barks. This is your call to action!

Instead of running to the crate room, however, you can walk now. Your puppy should be able to wait one to two minutes before going out to potty.

MILESTONES

Once your puppy is doing the following, you are ready for Phase 3:

1. Your puppy is sleeping through the night.

2. Your puppy is "holding it" four to six hours during the day.
3. Your puppy is training first and pottying second.
4. Your puppy is walking to the potty spot on their own (if this is feasible for your home setup).
5. Your puppy is telling you when they need to go potty.

In Phase 3, your puppy has more freedom. For this reason, it is important to make sure they are ready to leave Phase 2 before entering Phase 3. Remember, phases are based on abilities—age is merely a guideline.

PHASE 3: 16+ WEEKS OF AGE

In Phase 3, you are giving your puppy more off-leash freedom in the house. This comes in the form of tethered decompression (leashing your puppy to the place bed) and dropped-leash structure. You are trusting your puppy to not have an accident, but that does not mean you should not pay close attention to them. A sixteen-week-old puppy is still *very young*, but you should be starting to reap the rewards of your hard work from Phases 1 and 2.

DROPPED-LEASH FREEDOM

Give your puppy dropped-leash freedom in the house. Do they tell you when they need to go potty? Do they hold their bladder and wait to go potty outside? By now, they have gone potty outside more than a hundred times, so they should know where to pee and poop.

LIMIT ACCESS

Assume the best but prepare for the worst. Do not give your puppy access to rooms with white carpeting or irreplaceable rugs. Keep your puppy in the main rooms of the house, give frequent potty breaks, and continue building on their strong potty-training foundation! When in doubt or if you hit a few bumps in the road, go back to Phase 2.

WEATHER

As a reminder, you need to be taking your puppy out to potty in all types of weather. This not only teaches your puppy that weather does not matter, but it also teaches your puppy that they can and should go potty in all types of weather. If you are a fair-weather dog owner, you will create a fair-weather dog!

Rain, snow, sleet, all of it—take your puppy out to potty and stand out there with them. Lead by example.

TROUBLESHOOTING

If you are having major issues with potty training, check their medical first. Make sure your puppy does not have a urinary tract infection (UTI) or loose stool/diarrhea issues. Make sure they do not have a food intolerance. When in doubt, consult your veterinarian.

Chapter Summary

Potty training requires hard work and consistency, but when it is done right, it is a simple and straightforward process. Are you on Team No Accidents? I hope you are!

6.

CRATE TRAINING

"Good puppy training entails crate training."
—Amy Pishner

Crate training is something most puppy owners dread doing and fail to do correctly. They put their puppy in the crate, the puppy screams bloody murder, and they let them out. Fail.

"I tried crate training, and my dog hated it!"

The problem is not the crate itself—it's the approach. When used correctly, the crate is a safe space for dogs; they love it. You will learn to love it, too, when you follow my advice. The crate provides structure in your absence.

Crate training begins the first time you put your puppy in the crate. Granted, it might not be pretty, but you have to start somewhere.

In this chapter, I teach you how to properly crate train your puppy. I break it down into three phases just like potty training. I teach you everything you need to know to take your puppy from a screaming banshee to calm, cool, and collected in just eight weeks.

As your puppy matures, you will be able to phase out crate training. We use it to help with training, and then it can be eliminated when our dog no longer needs it.

Ready, set…CRATE!

CRATE BASICS

Let's review a few things before diving into Phase 1 of crate training!

CRATE SELECTION

By now, you should have a crate. Ideally, it's a plastic crate that is big enough for your puppy to stand up, lay down, and turn around in.

If you do not have a crate yet, go to Chapter 2, get a crate, and then come back to this chapter!

CRATE LOCATION

Location, location, location! It matters in real estate, and it matters for crates too. Your puppy's crate should be in a low-traffic room in your house that is free of distractions. I use my laundry room for my crate room. It is quiet, next to the back door where I take my puppy outside for potty breaks, and has a built-in fan for white noise (which I'll talk about next).

If you do not have a low-traffic room to use, a bathroom or closet will work just fine.

WHITE NOISE

White noise is critical. It helps drown out everyday noises around the crate room so your puppy can sleep soundly. If your puppy can hear everything that is going on around them, they will be waking up constantly and barking in the crate.

White noise can come from any source: a ceiling fan, a sound machine, a box fan, anything. It just needs to be loud enough to drown out the noise.

PHASE 1: 8–12 WEEKS OF AGE

In Phase 1, you are going to sync up what you do in potty training with what you do in crate training. This means you are paying close attention to your puppy's schedule so that you know when your puppy needs to go out and you are meeting your puppy's needs before putting them in the crate.

EXERCISE BEFORE CRATING

Do not put a hyper puppy in the crate. That puppy is going to scream bloody murder for a long time because they have the energy to do so. You *need* to exercise your puppy before putting them in the crate every single time in Phase 1.

Maybe this exercise is in the form of a potty walk, a play session with you or another dog, or a training session.

Always put a tired puppy in the crate for the best results!

COVER THE CRATE

Put your puppy in the crate, close the crate door, and then cover the crate with a towel, blanket, or sheet. This blocks visual stimuli and helps your puppy rest and relax.

CRATE DRILLS

In Chapter 8 (Obedience Training), I teach you all about crate drills. Crate drills teach your puppy to go into the crate on command, to wait patiently while the door is open, and to exit when you say "Free."

If you have a laid-back puppy, they will go into the crate easily for you. Some of you out there, though, have little velociraptors who are going to fight you every step of the way. It is going to be tough getting them into the crate. You have to be quick! Be patient. Your puppy will be working on crate drills soon enough. We need to cover some training groundwork first.

Once we start crate drills, put in the repetitions early on, and you will see a huge change in your puppy's overall attitude towards the crate. They are going to *love* it. They will be running into it on their own in no time.

"CALM BEHAVIOR GETS YOU OUT"

In Chapter 4, we talked about waiting until your puppy is calm to take them out of the crate. The same thing applies here in Phase 1. When you put your puppy in the crate, do not take them out—come hell or high water—until they are calm and quiet. Anything less, and you are teaching them to scream to get what they want. Once you go down that road, it is a slippery slope. You are going to kick yourself for not being firmer from the get-go.

Your puppy is screaming, not dying.

They are dramatic, but they are okay.

When you put your puppy in the crate, let them cry. As long as you took them potty and exercised them beforehand, you know that they are fine. No matter how long they scream the first week or so, their behavior is going to get better day after day and week after week. By week two, they should be quiet in the crate for the most part.

When your puppy gives up and falls asleep in the crate, be ready to give them a potty break as soon as they wake up.

GIVE THE DOG A BONE

Always give your puppy something to chew on in the crate. I leave a low-value deer antler in the crate for my puppy to chew on in case she is bored or not quite ready to take a nap. This bone helps prevent destructive behavior, such as chewing on the towel, and helps her settle down more quickly by giving her something to do.

MILESTONES

You should be able to say "Yes" to the following before moving on to Phase 2:

1. Your puppy goes in the crate willingly.
2. Your puppy settles quickly once in the crate.
3. Your puppy's whining or barking in the crate is minimal.
4. Your puppy chews on the bone in the crate if bored (you can hear them chewing it or see that the bone has been chewed).

PHASE 2: 12–16 WEEKS OF AGE

Once you have knocked out the milestones for Phase 1, you are well on your way to having a crate-trained puppy. Hooray!

For Phase 2, things get easier. You begin to ease up on things you were doing in Phase 1 because your puppy is maturing and does not need the extra help anymore.

Here are a few modifications for crate training in Phase 2.

COVER THE CRATE INTERMITTENTLY

Once your puppy learns to settle in the crate, you should not need to cover it every time. You can cover the crate in the mornings, when they have more energy, and in the afternoons if you think they need it. Outside of that, in the evenings, and especially when it is dark out, you should be able to leave the crate partially uncovered—maybe cover the sides but not the front.

USE WHITE NOISE INTERMITTENTLY

Just like covering the crate, you can start using white noise intermittently. This is because your puppy should be able to settle (and stay settled) without it. Turn it on only when you think your puppy needs it most.

A LITTLE NOISE IS OKAY

A little noise outside the crate room should be okay now. You should be able to talk normally, with or without the white noise on for your puppy, and your puppy should not react to your voice. Calm talking is best to make it easier on your puppy. If your puppy cannot handle it, turn the white noise back on.

WALK IN AND OUT OF THE CRATE ROOM

Walking into the room should not lead to your puppy throwing a fit and demanding to be let out. If it does, then you may need to go back to covering the crate and using white noise. For the most part, brief walk-ins should be no big deal for your puppy.

ELIMINATE THE TOWEL

If your puppy is not having accidents, remove the towel from the inside of the crate because they do not need it anymore. Resist the urge to put a dog bed in the crate in place of the towel. Your puppy is just fine laying in the crate with only a bone to chew on.

HOLDING IT LONGER

Potty training and crate training go hand in hand. As your puppy begins to hold their bladder longer, you should be able to start fading out using the crate for everything. They should be able to hang out on the place bed without problems and let you know when they need to go potty. Overall, they should be using the crate a little less each day. A potty-trained puppy has earned the privilege of more freedom inside the house and more freedom outdoors.

MILESTONES

Look for the following milestones before moving to Phase 3:

1. Your puppy is a star student in the crate (calm and quiet).
2. Your puppy does not need a cover or white noise anymore.
3. Your puppy is not having accidents in the crate or in the house.

PHASE 3: 16+ WEEKS OF AGE

Phase 3 means your dog is a rockstar in the crate and you are almost (but not quite) ready to start phasing out the crate. But wait! Do not eliminate it altogether and definitely do not throw it away. Continue using the crate sporadically so that your dog is comfortable in it should you need to use it in the future.

Here are a few things you can start doing in Phase 3.

CRATE ROOM FREEDOM

You can start phasing out the crate by giving your dog short periods of time alone in the crate room with the crate door open. Exercise them ahead of time, puppy-proof the room, and give them a few different bones to chew on.

Do this for five to ten minutes at a time.

PLACE BED IN PLACE OF THE CRATE

At this age, your puppy should be able to stay on the place bed, practicing tethered decompression training, for a few hours at a time. This means you can begin using the place bed in place of the crate. By doing so, you are continuing to provide structure without eliminating it altogether.

The place bed is a training tool that can be difficult to utilize properly. You will learn all about place bed training in Chapter 8.

SIZE UP

As your puppy grows, make sure the crate continues to fit them comfortably. I generally size up for most puppies once they reach around fourteen weeks of age and, by the time they are six months old, they are using an adult dog-sized crate.

TROUBLESHOOTING

If your puppy is having serious issues in the crate, there could be a number of things going wrong. Consult Chapter 14 (Problems and Solutions). Find the topic that best fits the problem you are having.

As for the rest of you, you should be seeing great success with your crate-training efforts by the end of Phase 2. By Phase 3, your puppy is well on their way to having off-leash freedom in the house.

Chapter Summary

Crate training is a worthwhile endeavor. By using the crate, you are helping to potty train your puppy, giving your puppy a chance to rest and relax, and creating a strong bond with them through structure and supervision. The crate is a godsend!

7.

BITING AND JUMPING

"Puppies will do what you allow them to do."
—Amy Pishner

Besides crate-training and potty-training struggles, the two chief complaints people have with their puppies are play biting (also called mouthing) and jumping up. Nobody's hands should look like they went through a meat grinder just because they own a puppy, and nobody likes being jumped on.

The good news is that biting and jumping are not complicated. They are easy behaviors to prevent and easy behaviors to fix.

Follow the tips outlined in this chapter and you will be on your way to having a well-mannered puppy in no time!

PUPPY BITING

In order to prevent your puppy from biting you, you have to understand why they are doing it in the first place. Let me break it down into bite-sized pieces (see what I did there?).

WHY PUPPIES BITE

Puppies bite because they have prey drive. Prey drive makes them want to bite anything that moves, which includes your hands, your pants, your shirt, your shoes, and anything else within reach. The more prey drive your puppy has, the more they want to bite!

That is the first reason why puppies bite. The second reason is that puppies explore with their mouths. Any time they are excited about something, they want to check it out, and they check it out by putting their mouth on it.

WHEN DO PUPPIES STOP BITING?

A lot of people incorrectly assume play biting stops at a certain age: "When my puppy is six months old, she will stop biting." That is not true at all! I have met three-year-old dogs who *still* mouth their owners and bite the leash because they were never taught not to.

Puppies stop biting when you make them stop.

Period.

Depending on the puppy's age at the onset of training, you can usually stop puppy biting altogether within about a week or two. It is not something that is meant to continue for weeks or months.

HOW TO PREVENT PLAY BITING

Preventing biting is the first step to stopping it. That is the honest truth.

Here are eight foolproof ways to prevent biting.

1. DO NOT WEAR LOOSE CLOTHING.

Shawls and dresses are an invitation for puppies to grab and bite clothing. Remember, prey drive is about moving objects. If your necklace is waving in front of your puppy's face, they are going to want to grab it. Young puppies have little to no impulse control.

2. DO NOT TEASE YOUR PUPPY WITH YOUR HANDS.

This is common sense, right? If you want your puppy to respect your hands, do not use them as a toy. Do not roughhouse with your puppy and then get mad when they latch onto your hand.

Instead, teach your puppy that hands are for holding and delivering food. It will change their thinking radically. This is yet another reason why training begins on day one!

If you want to play with your puppy, use a toy, never your hands.

3. DO NOT RUN FROM THEM.

Running incites prey drive. If you do not want your puppy to bite you, do not run from them. Prey drive makes puppies want to chase and bite moving objects. Rabbits run from wolves. Do not be a rabbit.

4. DO NOT SCREAM.

Along the lines of prey drive, screaming is literally the worst thing you can do with your puppy. When you run and scream, your puppy thinks you are prey! Be calm around your puppy instead.

5. TIRE THEM OUT BEFORE CUDDLING.

I know you want to cuddle your puppy. We all love puppy cuddles, but there is a time and place for everything. Do not attempt to cuddle your velociraptor puppy first thing in the morning when they are full of Red Bull. Wait until your puppy has had their needs met for physical exercise, mental stimulation, and training before you aim for cuddles. Cuddles at the end of the day are sweeter anyway!

6. HOLD THEM WITHOUT PUTTING YOUR HANDS IN THEIR FACE.

When you hold your puppy, face them away from you or to the side. Put one hand on their chest and the other on their back. This gives you control without putting your face or fingers in the line of fire!

7. GIVE THEM A BONE TO CHEW.

Make sure your puppy always has something to chew. This helps strengthen their jaw and cleans their teeth while satisfying their urge to bite. It gives them a productive outlet for their energy and is especially important during teething. (Teething starts at around four months of age.)

8. STAND UP!

Standing up is preferable to sitting down or getting on the ground with your puppy. When you get down at their level, you are at their mercy and are much less capable of protecting yourself. Your puppy is going to climb all over you and bite your hands, face, and hair. Only sit down with your puppy when they are calm and tired.

STOPPING PUPPY BITING

If you are following all the tips above and your puppy still bites you occasionally, do not fret. They are probably just an especially feisty or rambunctious puppy with higher prey drive.

Here are four proven methods to stop puppy biting.

1. "POP" THEM WITH THE SLIP LEAD.

If you want to stop puppy biting, keep your puppy on a leash at all times. This gives you full control over your puppy's movements and allows you to mitigate a bite before it happens. You can use the slip lead to give your puppy a quick "pop" before they bite you. A "pop" is a quick pull with the leash that gets your puppy's attention. It is not a yank or a drag or a slap—just a quick jerk of the leash.

2. SWAT YOUR PUPPY ON THE NOSE.

Have you ever seen a mother dog correct her puppies? It is a thing of beauty. *Nature at its finest.* A puppy's mom is their first teacher, and they expect that same level of leadership from you!

When we correct puppies for bad behavior, *it makes sense to them.* Puppies tend to get frustrated and confused when we do not correct them or if they are corrected inconsistently or incorrectly.

When a puppy bites incessantly on a momma dog, she nips them with her teeth, telling them to "Knock it off." When a puppy bites me, I tell them "No" and swat them on the nose. It is not a pat or a pet. It is a BOP. *Bam!* It hurts (a little) and surprises them (a lot). Even my protection puppies in training get bopped on the nose. They are smart and learn quickly when it is appropriate to bite and when it is not.

Correcting your puppy for biting will not hurt their feelings or cause them to dislike or distrust you. It is quite the opposite. Correcting your puppy teaches them to respect you and mind their manners!

3. STICK YOUR HAND IN THEIR MOUTH.

Another way you can correct a puppy who is biting your hand is by sticking your hand further into their mouth (and sideways) as they bite you. Hold it there for a second or two, press down on their tongue, which will probably make them gag a little, and then take your hand out of their mouth and present it to them again. If you did this right, they will definitely never bite your hand again.

This is a quick way to stop biting *and fast.* It is a more aggressive approach that is uncomfortable for the dog and highly effective.

You should only have to do it once (or twice, total) to teach your puppy the lesson: *"Bite me and I stick my hand in your mouth, which is very uncomfortable for you!"*

4. SCRUFF THEM.

This is the fourth and final option, and if you have come this far, then your puppy is having serious attitude problems. Chances are you have not done a great job setting them up for success.

But alas, if your puppy does not seem to be responding to methods 1–3 and you are giving swift and meaningful corrections, then scruff them. Grab them by the back of their neck, shake them for a quick second, and swat them on the nose while telling them in a loud, firm voice something like "*Knock it off!*" (It does not matter what you say as long as you sound serious.)

This gives the puppy a little reality check—*Mama's not happy*!

JUMPING

Ahh yes, jumping up. It might be cute when an eight-week-old *puppy* jumps up, but it is not cute when an eight-month-old *dog* does it.

Be fair to your puppy. Teach them from the get-go that jumping is a no-no.

Let's start by discussing why puppies jump.

WHY PUPPIES JUMP

Puppies jump when they are excited, when they want something, and when they are nervous. Three similar but different reasons. Regardless of the reason, jumping is disrespectful and should be stopped right away.

My rule from day one is "*Do not jump on me.*" As with biting, the best way to stop jumping is to prevent it in the first place.

PREVENTING JUMPING

Preventing jumping is simple when you follow the five tips below.

1. TEACH YOUR PUPPY THAT IN ORDER TO BE PETTED, THEY MUST SIT!

Teach your puppy that if they want attention from you, they need to sit first. Push their butt to the ground and lift their chin, then pet them. By doing so, you are shaping their sitting methods. Pretty soon, your puppy will begin sitting on their own prior to being petted.

2. USE THE LEASH.

It is really simple. If you do not want your puppy to jump on you, use the slip lead to stop them from jumping *the second they start to jump*. Do not wait until after your puppy has already jumped on you. It is too late at that point. The second their paws come off the ground, jerk the leash.

You will see me doing this occasionally during my personal program. I am communicating to Stella immediately and in a controlled manner that jumping is not cute and not allowed.

3. PUSH YOUR PUPPY'S BELLY WITH YOUR FOOT.

Another method is that when your puppy starts to jump on you, stick your foot out and push them backwards by the belly. They are going to fall flat on their face and, after that, they are going to think twice about jumping on you again. This is not mean. You are teaching your puppy that actions have consequences.

4. KNEE YOUR PUPPY IN THE CHEST.

If your puppy jumps on you, knee them in the chest—hard! I want them to fall back and reconsider their life choices. Seriously! It is a game-changer and, as realistically harsh as this may sound, your puppy has to fall. If you knee your puppy, and they continue to cling to your leg, you are doing it wrong. One swift jab should be all that is needed to get the desired result.

5. SWAT AT THEM.

If all else fails, when your puppy starts to jump on you, swat at them with your hand. They will learn to back off and give you space. You are not abusing your beloved pet! You are teaching them to be respectful in the most natural and humane ways possible.

GET OTHERS ON BOARD

You are responsible for your puppy's behavior around other people, but if your puppy starts to jump or bite and you alone are not able to stop it, ask people to help you out. Ask them to help correct your puppy for those bad behaviors by doing the same things you are doing. Teach them what to do. This will allow your puppy to learn to behave no matter who they are around because they will realize that everyone is on the same page about holding them accountable to the same rules. It is powerful and helps others enjoy your puppy without getting bit or jumped on.

Chapter Summary

Biting and jumping are easy to prevent and easy to correct. Both require consistency and a firm but fair attitude. Stick to your guns as your puppy's trainer and they will be well-mannered in no time.

8.

OBEDIENCE TRAINING

"A well-behaved dog in public is first a well-trained dog at home."

—Amy Pishner

By now we've covered the basics. You have the right puppy, the right equipment, and the right foundational knowledge to be a great dog owner. Now the fun begins!

In my online Puppy Head Start program, this chapter is a comprehensive and very successfuleight-week puppy obedience training course. It is the bread and butter of our program! Puppies learn dozens of basic skills and commands including Name Game, sit-stay, down-stay, Preheeling, place bed training, recall drills, crate drills, manners, and more!

In this chapter, I am going to highlight the most important canine skills and commands that your puppy needs to learn. I will tell you *what* to teach your puppy and *why.* Then I will share access to free training videos from my Puppy Head Start online course to give you a taste of how I train and help you get started with your dog at home. This training can be used on dogs of all ages. Foundation training is always the same no matter the dog's age, breed, or behavior. To access the videos, you can simply open your phone, scan the QR code below, and open the videos from our home page at www.valork9academyonline.com.

Happy training!

PREPARING FOR TRAINING

Before we start training, let's go over a few basic concepts to make sure we are on the same page. Review this information carefully.

THE PRIMARY TRAINER

As a reminder, there should be one person in your household who is primarily responsible for your puppy's training. This is the go-to person who reads the material, watches the videos, and applies the training. Everyone in the family is welcome to get involved, but there should be one person who takes full responsibility for the training outcome.

Who is your puppy's primary trainer?

THE TRAINING ROOM

You need a small, quiet, clutter-free room to train your puppy in. This is a space where your puppy can focus on you and ignore whatever is going on in the rest of the house. If you live alone, this can be any room you choose. If you have family members, it is best to pick a room away from the hustle and bustle.

I use my laundry room for puppy training. It is relatively small (twelve feet by eight feet) and has a large rug in it to keep my puppy from sliding around while training. The laundry room has a ceiling fan that I can turn on, if needed, to drown out the noise from the rest of the house. It is a great space to train in!

Where will you be training?

EQUIPMENT

For every training session, you will need your slip lead, treat pouch, and kibble. I recommend setting aside your puppy's allotted daily kibble in Ziploc bags to grab and go as needed.

You will occasionally use additional equipment, such as the crate or place bed.

PENCILING IN TRAINING

Your goal is to do five, five-minute sessions each day. This equals twenty-five minutes of total training each day. That said, when your puppy is young, you might do shorter sessions and train fewer times each day. Train *only* when your puppy is hungry and stop before they are full.

It is best to break up training throughout the day. I like to train in the mornings and afternoons and then set aside evenings for pack walks and playtime. This works well with my potty-training and crate-training schedules.

Plan your training sessions in advance until you are in the habit of working with your puppy throughout the day.

If you are ahead of schedule, that is great, but do not jump ahead. Instead, focus on more repetitions for your current week's homework.

If you are falling behind or need to take a week off, take your time and catch up. This training can be done at your own pace. But challenge yourself to stay on track! Your puppy's training will be most beneficial when it is done on a consistent, daily basis.

A GOOD TRAINING SESSION

On average, a good training session is five minutes long; however, with young puppies who are eight to nine weeks of age, you might opt to do sessions that are only one or two minutes long. Once your puppy is older, you can do longer sessions that are ten to fifteen minutes long or more.

If your puppy is not hungry and not wanting to work for food, stop training and try again the next day. You want your puppy to be hungry and motivated for food during your training sessions for optimal results.

During a given training session, work on anywhere from one to three different behaviors. This gives your puppy a variety of skills to work on and keeps them engaged. The goal is quality over quantity.

Keep your sessions short and sweet. End on a good note and have fun! The more *you* enjoy training, the more your puppy will enjoy it too!

No training is better than bad training. If you are hungry, tired, or irritable, do not train your puppy! Take care of yourself first so that you can bring your best self to each training session.

REVIEWING MARKER WORDS

We introduced marker words in Chapter 3. Let's do a quick recap!

We use three marker words:

- "Good" is the reward marker. It is followed by a food reward (R+).
- "No" is the correction marker. It is followed by restating the command or correcting the puppy (C+).
- "Free" is the release marker. It is followed by stepping back and giving the puppy a reward (R+).

Do not layer. Be sure to mark first, pause for a full second, then follow through. When saying marker words, do not add emotion or inflection to your voice. Keep your markers unemotional so that they sound the same each time you say them.

Emotion leaves room for interpretation, which can be confusing for puppies.

THE THREE Ds

Whenever we are working on a stationary behavior (like sit-stay or down-stay), we focus on teaching the behavior first. Next, we add duration, distance, and distractions (one at a time, in that order). Altogether, they are referred to as the three Ds. The end result is a very reliable "stay" behavior.

"NILIF"

Nothing in life is free. As you go through these eight weeks of obedience training, make sure your puppy is earning everything: food, praise, affection, belly rubs—you name it! We use rewards to our advantage to increase our dog's motivation to train, teach new behaviors, and help our dog make good choices.

At the onset of training, you may need to withhold food from your puppy for twelve to twenty-four hours. This fast will ensure that your puppy is hungry and motivated to train.

Your puppy will not die from missing a meal or two. However, *do not withhold water* during the fast. Let your puppy drink as much water as they want to.

It is important that you do not begin training if your puppy is not food-motivated. How do you know if they are food motivated? You offer them food. If they gobble it up, they are food-motivated. If they sniff it, lick it, or turn away from it, they are not food-motivated. (If your puppy is not food-motivated, go back to Chapter 3 and re-read "CMR: MOTIVATION.")

All dogs are food-motivated by nature. Use only kibble as your training reward over the next eight weeks and make sure your dog earns all the food they eat.

This is important!

If your puppy is not hungry after twenty-four hours of fasting, consult your veterinarian. There might be something medically wrong with your puppy and you need to get that figured out before any training begins.

STRUCTURE

With few exceptions, your puppy will not have off-leash freedom for the better part of the next eight weeks. Your goal is to shape good behavior by rewarding what you like and correcting what you do not like. This means you need to be present, have good timing, and provide structure for your puppy.

Your structure options for a young puppy are: tethering your puppy to you (keeping them on the slip lead with you), putting them in the crate (structure in your absence), and putting them on the place bed (tethered decompression).

Each of these are explained to you, step by step, in the course and will be reviewed in this chapter.

A FINAL WORD

Rome was not built in a day. Your puppy is not going to be a rockstar in one week. Be patient! Training is a marathon, not a sprint. Have fun and use this time to bond with your puppy. Training forges a lasting relationship between you and your new canine companion.

INTRODUCTION TO CANINE SKILLS AND COMMANDS

In this section, I will introduce the most important canine skills and commands that you can start working on with your puppy. As I mentioned earlier, I will teach you *what* to do and *why*, and then you can access my free Puppy Head Start course videos online so you can practice the behaviors at home with your puppy and purchase the full course if you wish to.

USING A SLIP LEAD

A slip lead is a combination leash and collar that is adjustable to any neck size. It is truly an essential piece of equipment.

From day one, I use a slip lead with every dog I train because it allows me to keep the dog with me, control the dog, and give direct feedback based on their behavior. When using a slip lead, you need to first determine if you want your puppy to walk on your left or right side. Commonly, dogs walk on the left side because, back in the day, hunters used to carry their rifles over their right shoulders, so they walked their hunting dogs on the other side. Your dog can walk on whichever side you like. I generally train dogs to walk on my left, but all of my personal dogs are "ambidextrous," meaning they can walk on either side of me.

If your dog will walk on your left side, you will put the slip lead in a "P" shape as you slide it over their head. If your dog will walk on your right side, it goes in the shape of a "q" as you slide it over their head. Always slide the leather tab down so it fits snugly against your dog's neck.

LURING

Luring is the first thing we teach puppies. Luring is a skill, not a command. It allows us to use positive reinforcement to shape behavior. You taught your puppy to find the food in your hand and to push into your hand for food in Chapter 4.

Now, we are going to use luring to teach straight lines and circles using both hands and going both directions. Remember to mark movement using the "Good" marker then follow through with a reward (R+).

Slow is smooth. Smooth is fast. Do not rush luring!

To teach straight lines, start by putting the piece of food in your right hand. Show the food to your puppy and when your puppy goes for it, take a small step back. Mark "Good" and reward your puppy with the piece of food. Continue this behavior until you are able to take several steps backwards while your puppy is pushing into your hand for the food. Always mark "Good" when you are moving, then reward your puppy.

You can repeat this same behavior with your left hand. Then switch to your right hand and practice moving forward with your puppy next to you—right hand first, then left hand.

As a reminder, you can access free how-to training videos directly from my course by visiting us online at www.valork9academyonline.com or by scanning the QR code below with your smart phone:

THE NAME GAME™

The Name Game teaches your puppy their name. It creates a positive association between your puppy's name and the reward and teaches them to make eye contact with you when you say their name.

Start by luring your puppy into a sit in front of you. Relax your hands at your side, say your puppy's name once, and wait for eye contact. When your puppy looks at you, mark "Good" and reward your puppy with a single piece of food. Repeat this exercise and keep the session short (about one minute).

If your puppy gets up, simply lure them back into a sit and start over. Do not tell your puppy to "Sit" or follow them around the room if they get up. Use your slip lead to keep them with you and use a food lure to put them back into a sit.

RECALL DRILLS™: RECALL RESET

Recall Drills teach puppies to come when called by making recall fun and rewarding.

The first Recall Drill that we teach is called "Recall Reset." It is simple, easy, and starts the conditioning process for the "Come" command.

Place a piece of food in your hand and move your hand in front of you, where your puppy is. Show your puppy the food and back up. As your puppy follows you, say "Come!" then praise them and give them the piece of food. Repeat this exercise a handful of times until your puppy is easily following you.

RECALL DRILLS™: 2-TREAT RECALL

2-Treat Recall is a very fun recall activity that gets your puppy running back and forth. It is the second Recall Drill in our lineup.

Take two pieces of food and throw one of them about three to five feet away from you. Allow your puppy to go get it, wait for your puppy to eat it, then say "Come!" As your puppy comes to you, back up a little, and reward your puppy with the second piece of food when they reach you.

Repeat this several times until your puppy is coming quickly when called. This is a nice exercise to do on rainy days or when your puppy has more energy to help tire your puppy out before doing more stationary obedience training drills.

CRATE DRILLS™

Crate Drills teach your puppy to enter the crate on command, wait while the door is open, and exit the crate on command. Crate Drills are truly a game-changer. They are difficult to do at first with most puppies, but the hard work pays off!

First, we motivate your puppy to go into the crate willingly and condition them using a food reward. To do this, open the crate door and toss a piece of food in front of the crate. Allow your puppy to eat the food and at the same time, toss a few more pieces directly into the crate. When your puppy is eating those, throw in some more. This will encourage them to stay in the crate while they get the food. Allow them to step out of the crate if they want to, but continue to toss more food into the crate for them to eat. They will quickly learn that if they stay in the crate, they get food.

Once your puppy catches on to the above, practice closing the crate door while sticking more food into the crate through the front or sides. When they are calm in the crate, begin opening the door slowly. If they try to rush out, shut the door and tell them to "Wait." When they are calm and still, open the door again a little bit at a time. When they no longer try to rush out of the crate, say "Free" and allow them to come out of the crate. Repeat until they understand very clearly what "Wait" means.

Very important: Once you start Crate Drills, be sure to reward your puppy each time they go into the crate throughout the day and practice "Wait" before allowing them out of the crate. This helps to create a positive association between the crate and the reward and enforces good crate behavior.

PREHEELING™

Preheeling is my foundation behavior for teaching "Heel." We teach puppies to walk next to us and sit when we stop by using a food reward. This helps stop leash pulling and shapes nice loose leash walking. Preheeling is magical and one of my favorite things to teach!

There are four steps.

- Step 1: Lure into heel position.
- Step 2: Reward for staying.
- Step 3: Take baby steps.
- Step 4: Try left/right turns and changing the pace.

We start by working on Steps 1–3. Lure your puppy into a heel position and have them sit. Mark "Good" and reward. Then reward your puppy for staying in heel position ("Good," reward). Lure your puppy as you walk, taking one step at a time, and when you stop, lure them into a sit, mark "Good," and reward. Once your puppy catches onto Steps 1–3, you can introduce Step 4 (trying turns and slow, fast, and normal paces)—all using a food reward.

ART OF DOING NOTHING™

The Art of Doing Nothing (AODN) is hands down one of my favorite things to teach dogs. It is a default behavior for the heel position. It teaches dogs to sit or lay next to us in heel without circling, pacing, whining, or jumping up.

Initially, teaching AODN can be challenging, but with practice, once your dog gets the hang of it, they will be a rockstar!

Start by luring your puppy into heel position next to you and into a sit. Mark "Good" and reward. Keep the leash short but not tight so that your puppy cannot get up and walk away. If they get up, use the leash to stop them and bring them back to heel position. They are allowed to sit or lay next to you. They cannot get up, crawl, lick, bite, paw at, or chew on anything around them. If they do any of these unwanted behaviors, correct them with the leash by giving it a quick "pop" and put them back into heel position. Do not reward undesirable behaviors. Reward only the behavior you like. If your puppy sits patiently next to you, you can reward them with food if you want to, but do so only occasionally and not often.

SIT-STAY

"Sit" means "Stay." The "Stay" is implied. This allows me to give one command without a hand signal, and my dog stays put until I release her ("Free!") or give another command (such as "Down," "Come," or "Heel").

To teach sit-stay, start by shaping the sit. With your puppy in front of you, take a piece of food and lure them into a sit by putting the food just over their nose and out of reach. Draw an arc with that food from your dog's nose to their forehead. They will follow the food with their head and end up in a sitting position. When they do, mark "Good" and reward. If they jump, stand, or try to turn with the food, simply reset and try again. You must be patient. Once dogs catch on, it is usually very easy to lure them into a sit again.

From there, you will want to begin shaping duration into your sit-stay. With your puppy in a sit in front of you, mark "Good" and reward them for staying. Then release them with the "Free" command, step back, and when they follow you, reward them with another piece of food.

The three Ds apply to sit-stay training too: duration, distance, and distractions. I teach them in that order. The end goal for a young puppy is a one-minute sit-stay, to the end of the leash, and with mild distractions. As your puppy grows older, you will be able to challenge them with a longer duration, more distance, and more distractions. Throughout each stay, I respond to eye contact by marking "Good" and rewarding. Eye contact is everything, and it is sewn into sit-stay training for a very impressive result!

DOWN-STAY

Down-stay is taught the same as sit-stay. "Down" means "Stay" and the "Stay" is implied. We start by shaping the down, building duration, adding the "Down" command, and then incorporating distance and distractions.

To shape the down, get down on your knees and lure your puppy in front of you. Lure your puppy by bringing the food towards their chest slowly then straight down to the ground. Many puppies stand up if you go too quickly or stay sitting if your lure is too far away. The goal is to find your puppy's sweet spot where they tuck their chin and follow the food to the ground.

Once your puppy is laying down, reward them heavily by marking "Good" and rewarding repeatedly with one piece of food each time. When you are ready for your puppy to stand up, mark "Free," pull your hand away, and reward your puppy for getting up.

Rinse and repeat. Once your puppy is easily luring into a down, you are ready to build duration and add the "Down" command. After that you will want to work on distance and distractions.

The hardest part of down-stay training is luring into the down and adding the "Down" command. Be patient as your puppy seeks to understand what you want them to do.

TETHERING

With eight-week-old puppies and for the first two weeks of puppy training, I carry puppies throughout the house. They do not walk on a leash inside the house and they do not get free time unsupervised in the house. This prevents unwanted chewing, fighting with the leash, and potty accidents in the house.

Once puppies are ten weeks old and after two weeks of training, I begin to give them downtime in the house via tethering. Tethering means putting a slip lead on your puppy and keeping your puppy with you at all times. When a puppy is tethered to me, I enforce the Art of Doing Nothing next to me when I am not moving around and I use Preheeling to move from point A to point B. I keep a treat pouch on me to reward good behavior and use the slip lead to correct unwanted behavior.

Think of the slip lead like an umbilical cord. It is a direct communication system between you and your puppy. Any time your puppy is out of the crate, they are learning. Tethering is a great way to teach calm behavior both on leash and in the house!

PLACE BED

The place bed is a client favorite! It is a raised bed with defined edges. Dogs can stand up, sit, and lay on it, but they cannot jump from it, bark from it, or get off of it. The place bed is a training tool for teaching dogs to be calm in the house and allows them to be in the room with us without getting underfoot.

To introduce the place bed to your puppy, start by flipping it over. Lure them onto it and reward them for standing on it. After they are comfortable with that, flip the bed back over and lure them on again and into a down position. Mark "Good" and reward them for being in a down.-

The command "Place" means to get on the bed, turn around, and lay down. After your puppy learns the "Place" command, you can start working on tethered decompression. Tethered decompression introduces duration. It helps puppies learn to settle on the place bed without whining or pacing.

To introduce tethered decompression, walk your puppy onto the place bed and then tie the leash to something behind them (such as a door handle or doorknob). Make sure the leash is snug enough to keep them from stepping off the bed but loose enough that they can comfortably lay down. Next, walk away from your puppy but stay in the same room. Ignore any whining or barking and wait for them to settle down and lay down. This could take thirty minutes or even an hour. For best results, exercise your puppy ahead of time and make sure that their food and potty needs have been met. I like to do tethered decompression in the evening after a long, busy day of exercise, play, and training.

Most puppies struggle with tethered decompression at first. Stay the course and do not give up! If you let your puppy off the bed when they are whining, they will learn that whining gets them what they want and that, my friend, is a slippery slope. The only time you will step in to correct your puppy will be for biting the leash or barking. Correct them with the leash, but other than that, leave them alone. Do not look at them or talk to them when they are whining.

A tired puppy is a good puppy! Once your puppy relaxes on the place bed, walk up and say "Free," then guide them off the bed.

Remember, when you are done using the place bed, prop it against the wall so your puppy cannot get on it. It is a training tool, not a lounge bed.

MANNERS

Manners matter. It is not enough for you to enjoy your puppy; other people should too! For this reason, I place huge emphasis on teaching puppies to have good manners around people, dogs, and at thresholds like the front door.

For me, a well-mannered dog in public sits next to its owner when people or other dogs approach. The dog does not leave position, does not jump up, and does not otherwise solicit attention. From here, the owner has the opportunity to give the dog permission to say hi if they choose to.

To begin teaching manners around people, lure your puppy into a heel position and a sit, and then mark "Good" and reward. Ask a friend or family member to help you by standing ten feet away or so. Ask them to approach slowly and calmly towards you and your puppy. When your puppy stays in position and is sitting, mark "Good" and reward. This teaches your puppy that sitting is a good thing and sitting is rewarded. If your puppy breaks and leaves the heel position, gets up, or barks at the person approaching, mark "No" and lure your puppy back into a heel position. Reward only the behavior you like. Correct the behavior you do not like.

It is important to allow only a small amount of slack in the leash during this exercise so that your puppy cannot get close to the person approaching. Ask the person to ignore your puppy and not give them any attention at first. This will help your puppy be calm and focus on you.

When it comes to manners with people, dogs (treated the same as people), and doorways (sitting as the door is opened and closed), practice makes perfect. The more you practice with your puppy, the better they will understand and the better behaved they will be!

When your puppy is ready for it, the cue to greet someone is "Go say hi." Encourage your puppy to keep "four on the floor," which means all four paws stand on the ground while they are being petted. If they jump, play bite, chew on the person's clothing, etc., use the leash to give a small correction and then bring them back to a heel position. Only good, calm behavior is rewarded with pets and affection.

Often, it is best to solicit help from calm family and friends before using excitable children or adults who lack self-control around puppies. You need your helper to help your puppy be successful and not cave to their cuteness!

THE ONLINE COURSE

The Puppy Head Start program is an eight-week course that teaches puppies obedience and manners from start to finish. This book only introduces the ideas. I included complimentary QR codes to access a handful of videos on our YouTube channel so you can see my training style and begin working with your puppy on a few behaviors at home. If you want to see how to teach the behaviors in their entirety, I would encourage you to check out our course. You will not be disappointed!

Chapter Summary

Great puppy training entails a step-by-step process of introducing behaviors and working on them. Keep in mind that as you work with your puppy at home, these taught behaviors are skills, each of which must be honed over a few weeks. They are not taught and finished in the same day. It is my hope that you are able to enroll in the Puppy Head Start course so that you can give your puppy a full eight weeks of obedience training for the best results!

I hope your puppy has enjoyed learning these new skills so far, and you have enjoyed teaching them. Remember, puppies are always learning, so do not stop here! The next chapters discuss socialization and exposure, physical exercise, mental stimulation, and more. Our goal is to raise a confident, well-mannered, and well-rounded canine companion.

9.

SOCIALIZATION AND EXPOSURE

"Having a go-anywhere, do-anything dog starts with socialization!"
—Amy Pishner

Socialization and exposure, collectively *socialization*, is one of the most overlooked aspects of puppy development. People focus so much on obedience and fail to realize that socialization is actually more important.

In this chapter, I take you step by step through the process of socializing your puppy. Using my system of Smart Socialization™, I break this down into seven categories and three phases to capitalize on each puppy's age and needs. Socialization goes hand in hand with obedience training (Chapter 8) and can be done on a daily and weekly basis with your puppy. It is a critical part of puppy training.

This chapter opens with owner education and then goes into detail about each of the phases and categories of socialization. A handful of free training videos are available to help you go through the material in this chapter. Simply click on the QR codes to access the videos.

OWNER EDUCATION

WHAT IS SOCIALIZATION?

Socialization is the process by which puppies become acclimated to their homes, their families, and the world around them. Socialization helps puppies adapt to change, builds their confidence, and minimizes anxiety while giving them a great quality of life.

Socialization is a critical aspect of puppy raising and requires an investment of time and effort.

THE SEVEN CATEGORIES OF SOCIALIZATION

The VK9 Method is comprised of *seven* different categories of socialization and exposure. These categories provide your puppy with the experiences they need to be a confident dog. Let's go through them one by one!

CATEGORY 1: PEOPLE

Your puppy needs to meet people: big people, small people, old people, young people, loud people, quiet people, tall people, short people, people of different races and ethnicities, and kids. Lots and lots of kids.

CATEGORY 2: PLACES

Your puppy needs to go to new places: the hardware store, home improvement store, gardening center, outdoor markets, inactive and safe construction zones, friends' houses, and more. Anywhere your puppy can safely and legally go, they need to go.

CATEGORY 3: SIGHTS

Your puppy needs to see new things: umbrellas, flags, crutches, wheelchairs, bikes, brooms—you name it. The more your puppy sees, the more they normalize.

CATEGORY 4: SOUNDS

Your puppy needs to hear new sounds: blenders, gunshots, fireworks, vacuum cleaners, leaf blowers, lawn mowers, saws, motorcycles, and crying babies. As with sights, the more your puppy hears, the more they normalize.

CATEGORY 5: SURFACES

Your puppy needs to explore new surfaces: stairs, hardwood floors, carpet, tile, vinyl, tarps, obstacles, see-through surfaces, metal surfaces, slippery surfaces, wobbly surfaces, narrow surfaces, swinging surfaces, and swaying surfaces.

Socialization on surfaces plays a major role in overall environmental soundness. It is a super easy category to knock out at home.

CATEGORY 6: ANIMALS

Your puppy needs to meet new animals. These can be animals your puppy interacts with, such as other dogs, and animals your puppy does not need to interact with, like cattle, horses, chickens, and cats.

Puppy play and playing with other dogs is so important that I dedicate Chapter 12 to this particular topic.

CATEGORY 7: EXPERIENCES

This category is specific to The VK9 Method. I created it as a sort of umbrella policy to cover items not mentioned in the first six categories. It includes staple items like bathing, brushing, nail trims, and car rides, and includes bonus items like pack walks, hiking, after-dinner dance parties, and cuddling on the couch.

Experiences is an open-ended category. Think of the life you want to have with your puppy. What does it include? *What do you want to do with your puppy now or in the future?*

Will you be taking your dog boating with you? How about standup paddleboarding? Is your dog going to fly on a plane or go swimming in the lake? Will your dog go to kids' birthday parties? What about road trips?

Put it all on the list! This is where you get to tailor your puppy's training to your lifestyle. Socialization should never be cookie-cutter. Every person, family, and lifestyle is different. Customization is important!

THREE METHODS OF SOCIALIZATION

Now let's talk about *how* to properly socialize your puppy. There are three methods of socialization: positive, neutral, and negative.

POSITIVE SOCIALIZATION

Positive socialization is when something good happens in the presence of something new. It is when your puppy receives positive reinforcement (rewards) during socialization. This creates a positive association between the new experience and the reward.

Examples include being pet gently by a stranger, getting food, praise, and affection from their handler on a new surface, playing harmoniously with kids, and playing nicely with another dog.

NEUTRAL SOCIALIZATION

Neutral socialization is when nothing good or bad happens in the presence of something new.

Examples include passing a dog on the street, walking on a hardwood floor, seeing a wheelchair, and watching kids play–without rewards or fanfare.

NEGATIVE SOCIALIZATION

Negative socialization is when something bad happens in the presence of something new. Negative socialization is something we try to avoid because it is not ideal. A little stress is fine, but too much stress is not a good thing.

Examples include your puppy getting attacked by another dog, something falling on your puppy, kids pulling on your puppy's fur, someone stepping on your puppy's tail, someone mistreating your puppy in another way, or your puppy falling off a new surface.

Now, let's talk about a few more terms and definitions related to socialization.

STARTLE RECOVERY RESPONSE

Let's say something bad or scary happens. Your puppy has what we call a startle recovery response (SRR). It determines how quickly your puppy can recover from something that startles them. At the core of it is emotional resilience.

Let's say your puppy is tethered to you in the kitchen while you empty the dishwasher. You accidentally drop a metal spatula next to your puppy, and it lands on the floor with a loud bang. Your puppy gets startled and runs to the other end of the leash.

That is a normal response because puppies are all about survival. It is what happens next that I care about the most.

A puppy with a good SRR will pause, consider what just happened, and come back to you.

A puppy with a great SRR will come back quickly, investigate the spatula, and maybe even play with it.

A puppy with a poor SRR will not come back to you, no matter what, and they will probably avoid that part of the kitchen for several days—even after the spatula is long gone.

Genetics plays a major role in determining a puppy's instinctual SRR. A well-bred puppy is confident and recovers quickly from anything that startles them. Well-bred puppies have great SRRs.

Training can improve a puppy's SRR, but it will not change it completely.

EUSTRESS

Did you know there are two types of stress? *Eustress* is a positive kind of stress. *Distress* is a negative kind of stress.

"Eustress" is a Greek word. The prefix "*eu*" means "good" or "well," and "*stress*" refers to any type of change that triggers strain.

In socialization, the goal is to provide your puppy with positive and neutral socialization experiences, but that does not mean everything has to be easy for your puppy.

In certain situations, it is helpful to provide your puppy with good stress (*eustress*), so your puppy can learn how to handle stress and become more confident because of it.

Stress is not necessarily bad. It is a part of life. Teaching your dog to cope with stress enhances their resiliency and creates a bombproof companion.

SOCIALIZATION PERIODS

There are two socialization periods you need to know about.

THE CRITICAL SOCIALIZATION PERIOD

The *critical socialization period* (CSP) is from roughly three to sixteen weeks of age. It is during this limited time in your puppy's development that anything they experience once or twice in a positive way is something they will be comfortable with for the rest of their life.

Because this period starts at three weeks of age, breeders, rescues, and shelters have a major impact on it. Reputable breeders invest the necessary effort into providing *early neurological stimulation* (ENS), as well as playpens and new sights, sounds, and surfaces for their puppies to explore and experience. They allow their puppies to spend time with safe adult dogs, and they welcome adults and children to come over and help socialize their puppies.

Puppies coming from reputable breeders are blessed with a jump-start on their socialization. Good breeders really do not get enough credit for everything they do to provide top-quality puppies to their buyers.

Most puppies go to their new homes between eight to nine weeks of age. This means you have seven to eight weeks to finish out your puppy's CSP. It may seem like a lot, but the time goes by quickly!

By the time your puppy reaches sixteen weeks of age, their best opportunities for socialization and confidence building are over. You cannot go back in time and no amount of training will make up for missed experiences during this ever-important period.

THE SOCIALIZATION WINDOW

Your puppy's overall *socialization window* is from birth to twelve months of age. If you failed to socialize them early on or you adopted an older puppy, you can still play a little bit of catch-up.

Socialization can and should continue through adulthood. Any socialization done within the first year of a dog's life has a lasting impact. The only difference is, the older the puppy is, the less impactful socialization is.

A WORD ON PARVOVIRUS

Parvovirus (also called "parvo") is an infectious DNA virus that commonly causes severe illness in young and unvaccinated dogs. It can be deadly, especially for puppies exposed under eight weeks of age.

Signs and symptoms of parvo include fever, diarrhea, vomiting, lethargy, shivering, weight loss, and not eating or drinking.

Most veterinarians say that in order to keep puppies safe from parvo, it is best to keep them at home until after they have had all their shots.

This is true, but *it is also bad advice.*

If you keep your puppy at home until they have had all their shots, they will be around sixteen weeks of age. That means by the time you go on your first field trip, your puppy's critical socialization period will already be over. As a result, your puppy will stand a good chance of being fearful *for life*.

I repeat—do not keep your puppy in the house until after they have had all their shots. It is a mistake!

Socialize your puppy, but be *smart* about it!

SMART SOCIALIZATION™

Smart Socialization entails avoiding areas that might be contaminated with parvo and keeping your puppy away from other unvaccinated dogs.

Parvo is transmitted through feces and can live in the ground for up to seven years. For this reason, you want to avoid dog parks, pet stores, grassy areas outside of pet stores and pet-friendly stores, and any other areas where unknown dogs pee and poop.

Parvo can also live on concrete and other hard surfaces. To keep your puppy safe, carry them through stores and parking lots until they've had their second puppy shot.

Smart Socialization makes it easy to socialize your puppy and feel good about it! Everything I do while socializing puppies takes these safety measures into consideration.

VACCINATIONS

Puppies who are nursed by a mother dog that was vaccinated against parvo receive antibodies from their mother's milk. From there, puppies receive shots to help increase the antibodies their bodies need.

Typically, puppies receive distemper and parvovirus shots around six to eight weeks of age. Around ten to twelve weeks of age, they receive the DHPP shot with vaccines for distemper, adenovirus (hepatitis), parainfluenza, and parvovirus (DHPP). Around sixteen to eighteen weeks of age, they receive another DHPP shot.

I personally prefer for my puppy to get the first shot at eight weeks old, the second one at twelve weeks old, and the third one at sixteen weeks old so that there is a full four weeks between shots. This allows me to spread out shots as much as possible.

Be sure to do your due diligence regarding vaccinations. Many veterinarians will recommend additional vaccinations and booster shots that are optional and not necessary for puppies and can do more harm than good, especially when given in conjunction with other vaccines.

FEAR PERIODS

When puppies are young, the brain undergoes a rewiring and integration process called *pruning*. This is when neural circuits that are not being used are thrown away and new circuits are linked, protected, and upgraded for maximum efficiency.

During this complex process, there is sometimes a temporary decrease in capability and some processing mistakes may be made. We call these mistakes *fear periods*.

There are two fear periods. The first one happens at around eight weeks of age. The second happens around eight months of age, give or take a few months.

Some puppies experience one fear period; others experience both. Some puppies experience none at all. There is a good chance your puppy will not experience a fear period, but do not count on it. It has nothing to do with genetics and everything to do with luck!

Fear periods can last a day, a week, a few weeks, or even a few months.

During a fear period, puppies act fearfully towards things they previously were not afraid of: a specific person or people in general, a specific place or places in general, sights, sounds, surfaces, that chair sitting in the corner of the room that hasn't moved in months, dogs, cats, car rides, etc.

The fears are random and do not have any basis in reality or the socialization that has been done thus far in the puppy's life. There is no reason for any specific fear during a fear period.

Fear periods are developmentally normal, although they can be alarming.

My German shepherd, Havok, went through a fear period when he was eight and a half weeks old. For one whole day, he was afraid of other dogs. The next day, he went back to normal and loved other dogs.

That is how fear periods work. The tricky part is that it can be difficult to identify a fear period in a young puppy who is eight weeks old if you did not previously evaluate that puppy at seven weeks of age.

(This is why temperament testing is so important!)

With older puppies, if you have had the puppy for several months, fear periods are much easier to identify. If your confident puppy is suddenly fearful, it is a fear period.

What should you do if your puppy is in a fear period? Absolutely nothing. The best thing to do during a fear period is *nothing*. Keep your puppy at home and ride it out. Avoid whatever frightens them.

Do not try to work your puppy through their fear. They are not real fears; they are not a fearful puppy. They are a normal, confident puppy who is going through a fear period. Their brain is temporarily disconnecting and rewiring.

If you force your puppy to face their fears during a fear period, you can do permanent damage and create lifelong aversions.

Stop socializing. Pause your field trips. Keep your puppy at home and focus on obedience and relationship building instead.

When in doubt, consult a professional. We have experience with fear periods and can help you identify if your puppy is in one and coach you through it.

The important thing to remember is, fear periods do not last forever. Your puppy will go back to normal soon.

Now, let's get into the hands-on portion of this chapter!

SOCIALIZATION PHASES 1, 2, AND 3

I am breaking up socialization and exposure into three phases. Each phase has its own set of instructions, checklists, and goals. Each phase is based on your puppy's age, immunity, mental development, and training objectives.

If you are starting this chapter with an older puppy, you need to literally double down on socialization. Socialization is *goals-based* and *age-based.* It is time-sensitive. If your puppy is more than twelve weeks of age right now, you need to move twice as quickly through the material as you normally would. That means you have *one week* for Phase 1 and *one week* for Phase 2. You *need* to start Phase 3 before your puppy is no more than fourteen weeks of age so you can finish it before the critical socialization window closes. This is important!

If you have an older puppy who has not yet been socialized, cancel your plans—you have training to do!

To watch a summary video of Socialization Phases 1–3, you can visit my website at www.valork9academyonline.com or scan the QR code below.

SOCIALIZATION PHASE 1: AT HOME (8–10 WEEKS OF AGE)

In Phase 1, we take it easy. Your puppy has just experienced a lot of change by leaving their breeder or rescue and coming home with you. We do not want to overwhelm them by doing too much, too soon. Let your puppy settle in, get to know you, and begin bonding with you.

Everything in Phase 1 happens at home and on your immediate property. You do not leave home with them.

Here are the seven categories of socialization with instructions on how to approach each one. Note: When working with your puppy, cover only one to two things at a time and no more than a few things each day. You want to break these up into doable, bite-sized pieces for your puppy.

Less is more.

PHASE 1 PEOPLE

Goal: 4+ new people

During Phase 1 People, I want your puppy to meet four or more new people. These people can be immediate household family members, extended family, friends, neighbors, and guests.

Introduce one person at a time. Ask the person to be calm and sit down somewhere accessible to the puppy. Put your puppy down on the ground and allow the person to call them. *It is your puppy's choice to approach or not.* This is important!

Most puppies will happily run up and receive all the love a new person has to offer. Once your puppy settles in, it is okay for the person to pick them up if they want to. Just make sure your puppy is held securely so they do not fall. I like to hold puppies on their backs, cradled in my arm or under my arm in a football carry.

If your puppy jumps up or play bites, step in and correct them. Wait for them to calm down before allowing the person to pet them again.

Keep the meeting short so your puppy does not get wound up, and try to end on a good note when your puppy is calm, well-behaved, and having a good time

Praise and affection are sufficient rewards to make meeting new people a positive experience for your puppy.

PHASE 1 PLACES

Goal: At home only, inside and outside the house

During Phase 1 Places, your puppy stays home with you. This makes it easy. Do not worry—there is plenty to explore! Each new room in your house is a new place as far as your puppy is concerned. Your yard is full of fun things to check out as well. I like to use food to reward my puppy for confidence and good behavior.

It is important to note that your puppy should be kept on a leash to sightsee inside the house. You lead your puppy into each new room and reward your puppy for checking it out. It is okay to keep lights turned off and allow your puppy to walk into darkened rooms. This builds confidence.

PHASE 1 SIGHTS

Goal: 4+ new sights

Break out the kibble—it is going to come in handy. When exposing your puppy to new sights, there are things that are just part of your home and décor that your puppy will see naturally on a day-to-day basis. There are also things that are a little out of the ordinary that you will intentionally expose your puppy to, such as an umbrella. Use lots of rewards to make these experiences fun for your puppy. Allow your puppy to explore new sights on their own. Reward curiosity.

PHASE 1 SOUNDS

Goal: 4+ new sounds

Much like with sights, you are going to use lots of rewards to expose your puppy intentionally to new and different sounds that are unusual to your home. For many of these, it will be a good idea to exercise your puppy ahead of time so that they can better handle the small amounts of stress these sounds might present to them.

Use rewards and movement to make this socialization fun. Always reward your puppy both for being curious and for focusing on you. For loud sounds, start a good distance away so you can mitigate your puppy's stress level. You do not want to start with something too loud or be too close. This can cause your puppy to startle, and, if their SRR is not good, they may not recover. Distance is your friend.

PHASE 1 SURFACES

Goal: 4+ new surfaces

Surfaces is a fun one! You want to pick out new surfaces from the list to intentionally expose your puppy to. Initially checking out the new surface is enough to warrant a reward (usually food paired with praise and affection). After doing so, wait for your puppy to put a single paw on the surface, then eventually both front feet and both back feet, and finally walk across it.

My goal when exposing a puppy to a new surface is to start where I can, make some progress, then end on a good note. I can always come back to that new surface later and pick up where I left off. Resist the urge to be greedy and ask for too much at once.

PHASE 1 ANIMALS

Goal: Safe pack members only

Patience is a virtue. I am telling you this because I know what people love to do when they get a new puppy. They want to bring the new puppy home and introduce them to their pack right away. This brings a lot of excitement into the mix and can be overwhelming for the puppy.

I say wait a few days instead. Give your puppy time to settle in, get comfortable, get to know you, and meet the human family members first. It is important for your puppy to feel safe, and this period of time (just a few days) allows your other dogs to acclimate to the newest pack member as well.

You can carry your puppy around the other dogs; just do not put them down with them. After a few days, you can introduce them to each other—starting with your oldest and calmest pack member first. Exercising your dogs prior to introducing them to your puppy is always a good idea!

After the dogs are introduced, we go on lots of pack walks together during Phase 1 Animals. I do not encourage (or allow) my adult dogs to play with the young puppy right away. I want everyone to learn to be neutral together first. Pack walks help tremendously with this.

This sets the tone for their relationship together and builds the puppy's confidence.

It is important for very young puppies to feel safe and get space when they are around other dogs. They are *learning* how to socialize. Every interaction matters.

If you do not have any other dogs in the house, that is fine. In that case, you can skip this category for Phase 1. It is better to introduce your puppy to *no* dogs than introduce your puppy to dogs you do not know well or dogs who may not be puppy-friendly.

If you have other dogs that are not friendly, do not introduce them to your puppy in Phase 1. It is better to be safe than sorry.

PHASE 1 EXPERIENCES

Goal: 4+ new experiences

This is another fun one! Phase 1 Experiences is where I get to start introducing my puppy to what life is like with me and my family. I also introduce grooming! I usually do these things in the evenings after exercise, when my puppy is tired. I use whatever rewards are most effective for that individual experience or no rewards at all if rewards cause my puppy to get excited during a time when I want them to be calm. Sometimes no reward is the best reward, but it just depends.

Examples of experiences: car rides, nail trims, grooming, camping, boating, hiking, walking alongside a bicycle, running alongside a quad or ATV, cuddling on the couch, hometown parades, travel, dog shows, dog sports, and other pet-friendly activities. Keep in mind that your puppy will be too young for some of these, but as your puppy matures and makes their way through socialization, be sure to touch on any topics that apply to your lifestyle.

No other dog trainer talks about experiences as a category of socialization, and I just think it is so important! If you want your puppy to adapt to your lifestyle, you must *show* them what your life is like!

PHASE 1 SUMMARY

You have two weeks and lots to accomplish. The good news is, each one only takes a few minutes to do and you can easily fit them into your daily schedule. It is a good idea to plan ahead and pencil in your daily and weekly socialization goals so you will know what needs to be done and you will not fall behind.

SOCIALIZATION PHASE 2: AT HOME AND IN TOWN (10–12 WEEKS OF AGE)

During Phase 2, you continue working on things at home and plan a few field trips into town. These are Smart Socialization™ field trips and visits to friends' houses.

Your puppy continues working for all of their food, and you use food as a reward during socialization. Nothing in life is free, remember?

PHASE 2 PEOPLE

Goal: 16+ new people

That's right, sixteen or more! This is where we really start doubling down on socialization with people. This socialization can be direct (actually meeting someone) or indirect (just seeing someone). This makes your life easier and will help you accomplish that goal of sixteen or more easily in two weeks' time.

When introducing your puppy to someone, follow the same protocol as Phase 1. Keep it positive (food, rewards, affection, all good things) and make sure your puppy is the one that approaches first to say hi, not the other way around. This rule applies to kids too. Your puppy approaches *first.*

Ask people to be calm, and introduce one person at a time. Allow your puppy to say hi, get all the love, and then come back to you to reset before meeting more new people.

PHASE 2 PLACES

Goal: 8+ new places

Load up the car—it is time for field trips! You are going to start taking your puppy to new places. Carry them if you can, or put them in a cart or stroller. In this phase, their paws do not touch the ground (with the exception of potty breaks in Smart Socialization™ spots).

As you go to new places, let your puppy take it all in. Pet them calmly and avoid chaotic spots like tight crowds, loud kids, and barking dogs. You want these experiences to be positive. Feel free to give your puppy food, but, for the most part, let this socialization be neutral. Neutral is okay.

Phase 2 People marries up with Phase 2 Places because your puppy is going to see lots of new people on their excursions.

PHASE 2 SIGHTS

Goal: 4+ new sights

This is an easy objective, and you have plenty of time to accomplish it. You did great work during Phase 1 Sights. We are building on that in this phase. Use rewards to make new sights positive for your puppy and try to always end on a good note. Socialization is fun!

You should start to see your puppy embracing new sights with more confidence and curiosity. That is a telltale sign that your hard work is starting to pay off!

You are bound to run into new sights in town, but for the most part focus on introducing your puppy to new sights at home in your controlled environment.

PHASE 2 SOUNDS

Goal: 4+ new sounds

Just like Phase 2 Sights, you can do Phase 2 Sounds at home to control the sounds used and your puppy's reaction to them. Use a food reward and start incorporating your puppy's obedience training into socialization. Do something simple like luring to keep your puppy's focus on you while exposing them to new sounds. Distance is your friend, especially with loud sounds like leaf blowers.

Pro Tip: Dogs do *not* have to be afraid of fireworks, thunder, or gunshots. With proper exposure, they can learn to be calm and confident around any sound. One of my favorite things to do during Phase

2 Sounds is to introduce puppies to loud or startling noises—like gunshots or fireworks—in a controlled, low-pressure way. I will play recordings from my phone or computer at a low volume during training sessions, gradually increasing the volume over time. This kind of intentional, structured exposure helps desensitize puppies and build their confidence. Instead of reacting fearfully, they learn that loud noises simply mean it is time to focus, play, or work. It is a simple step that pays off for life.

PHASE 2 SURFACES

Goal: 8+ new surfaces

You are hitting the ground running with this one. Remember how I said that new surfaces are a cornerstone for confidence building? Your work in this phase is going to help significantly with field trips in Phase 3! Go the extra mile to make sure you reach this goal. It will pay dividends later!

PHASE 2 ANIMALS

Goal: 6+ new animals

In Phase 2 Animals, I want you to look for new animals to introduce your pup to. If you do not have dogs at home, then you need to set up a playdate or two to introduce your puppy to other safe, social dogs. If that is not an option, do not worry about it for now, but it *needs* to happen in Phase 3. No exceptions! Plan accordingly.

My other young dogs are now allowed to play with Stella, and she is loving every second of it. She is confident, feels at home with us, and play sessions are teaching her how to communicate with other dogs. Be sure to check out Chapter 12 (Puppy Play) for more on this topic!

PHASE 2 EXPERIENCES

My favorite list again! This is the one I look forward to the most because it is an opportunity to continue acclimating my puppy to life at my house and overall pack life with the Pishners. Phase 2 Experiences can be a repeat of Phase 1 Experiences, but look to advance in each activity with your puppy. Your puppy is now riding in the car crate, getting a full bath, learning to walk on the treadmill, getting their nails trimmed, and more.

You are habituating your puppy to your home and your pack, and you are teaching them what your expectations are for them. Be a good leader throughout Phase 2 Experiences, and your puppy will adapt quickly!

PHASE 2 SUMMARY

Are you keeping up? If you are knocking out your goals, you are going to be amazed at *just how awesome* your puppy is at only twelve weeks old!

You are bonding with your puppy through quality training and socialization, and they are getting invaluable life experiences and socialization opportunities.

Good work! Let's keep it going in Phase 3.

SOCIALIZATION PHASE 3: FIELD TRIPS (12–16 WEEKS OF AGE)

Get ready to hit the town! Phase 3 is all about field trips. Your puppy's obedience training starts paying off, and you get to show your puppy the good world!

Phase 3 is absolutely critical to your puppy's development. Do not overlook it. Do not be lazy. *And do not skip anything.*

Once your puppy reaches sixteen weeks of age, the critical socialization window closes, and your chance to solidify positive first impressions about things is over. If your puppy has not seen something by sixteen weeks of age, there is a good chance they could show a fear response to it.

Field trips, field trips, field trips. That is what Phase 3 is all about! This Phase has just four categories: field trips (which encompasses places, sights, sounds, and surfaces), people, animals, and experiences.

PHASE 3 PEOPLE

Goal: 16+ new people

Yes, a lot of people! You are going to have to be *social* with your dog. If you are an introvert like me, I apologize in advance! You need to step out of your comfort zone. Phase 3 People includes introducing your puppy to men, women, children, babies, elderly people, and people of all ethnicities. With all of these, your puppy's experiences need to be *positive*. They need to experience something *rewarding* like food, praise, pets, affection, or playtime when meeting new people. The reward can come from you or from the other person.

Taking your puppy to the park during a busy time is a great way to introduce them to kids. Smile, be approachable, and make sure your puppy minds their manners.

With babies, the goal is to have your puppy around babies who fuss and cry. This helps to desensitize them to those noises and habituate them to kids of all ages.

PHASE 3 FIELD TRIPS

Goal: 16+

Instead of doing individual categories for places, sights, sounds, and surfaces, I merge everything into one category to make your life easier: field trips. On field trips, you can knock out everything your puppy needs to see and do. (Two birds, one stone!) The only thing you do not do in Phase 3 Field Trips is introduce your puppy to people. This is because you now want your puppy's focus to be on you—and no one else. We reserve socialization with people for separate socialization sessions.

In Phase 3 Field Trips, you need to take your puppy everywhere they can legally go. Their immunity to parvo and other diseases is high. It is time to hit the road!

Exercise your puppy before field trips and make sure they have a good appetite. Use your car crate for transportation, and reward good focus, confidence, and obedience to commands at each location.

Get your puppy's focus right away and engage them. Engagement in new locations is key! Do easy things like luring, the Name Game, and Preheeling to reward your puppy for good obedience.

Walk with confidence. Head up! Shoulders back! Your puppy is watching you and mirroring what you do. If you want a confident puppy, you need to be a confident handler.

On your field trips, take any opportunity you can to present your puppy to new sights, sounds, and surfaces. However, be respectful of pet-friendly stores and *never* put your puppy on retail items or goods that could be damaged by their nails. Pet-friendly stores are a privilege, not a right.

PHASE 3 ANIMALS

Goal: 16+

Your puppy will be sixteen weeks old at the end of this phase, so we are really doubling down on socialization with animals. Your goal for Phase 3 Animals is to set up lots of playdates with other dogs. Your puppy needs to practice playing with dogs of different ages, sizes, play styles, energy levels, and temperament types.

I recommend staying away from dog parks, and do not let your puppy play with dogs that might not be friendly. Bad experiences could set you back—you do not want that! Never introduce your puppy to aggressive dogs, reactive dogs, or random dogs in public.

Be sure to look at Chapter 12 for more information. I teach you how to introduce your puppy to other puppies and dogs and discuss the importance of reading body language.

Additionally, in this phase, you put your obedience to the test and introduce your puppy to animals of other species like cows, chickens, cats, and horses. This means you might have to make friends with farmers. I have reached out to complete strangers before to ask if I can socialize my puppies around their horses, and they have always said yes. (I am grateful to them!) Find a way to access different animals. It is worthwhile!

If you are having a hard time finding puppies and dogs for your puppy to socialize with, you need to think outside the box. Go online and find social media groups and people in your area. Ask people to meet up with you. Contact trainers and ask about playdates for dogs or pay to board your dog with a reputable trainer so your puppy can socialize with their pack. We do this all the time for clients!

PHASE 3 EXPERIENCES

Goal: Continue Phase 1 and 2 Experiences and add some new ones!

In Phase 3, you are building on the experiences your puppy had in Phases 1 and 2. You are continuing to set your pup up for success by tiring them out ahead of time, using a food reward, being their leader, and thinking ahead to line up new opportunities for them.

Remember, the question you want to ask yourself is: "What do I want to do with my puppy in six months or a year?" Do you want your pup to go swimming at your lake cabin? Do you plan to fly with your dog? Do you love boating? Those are all great experiences for your puppy to have *now* so that they can enjoy them *later* too!

Try to accomplish each item on the checklist more than once—weekly, if possible—so that your puppy has multiple positive experiences in their memory bank. Your puppy is only this young once. Make it count!

PHASE 3 SUMMARY

Phase 3 is a fun but time-consuming phase. You are heading into town often and planning lots of fun activities for your pup to see, hear, and take part in. Try to do things more than once and have fun with it! Your puppy is always learning, and the more you do now, the more you will not have to do in the future.

Twelve to sixteen weeks of age is a critical period of time in your puppy's growth and development. Take advantage!

TROUBLESHOOTING

Is your puppy struggling with something? Perhaps your puppy is having a hard time with people, is not comfortable in new places, shies away from new sights, or is sound-sensitive.

Maybe you have a genetically more nervous dog or your pup had bad experiences before you started this training program. Keep the faith! There are lots of things you can do to tackle socialization from different angles.

Here are a few pro tips!

1. Distance is your friend. If there is ever anything your pup is afraid of, start further away from it and then incrementally get closer—within that same session or from session to session.
2. Movement is motivating. Do not let your puppy stop and stare at whatever is making them nervous. Keep moving! Movement is motivating. Movement stops them from fixating on their fear.
3. Keep sessions short. Do not ask for too much in any given session. Work with your puppy for just a few minutes at a time when introducing something new.
4. End on a good note. This one is critical! If your puppy is making progress, stop while you are ahead. Take your win and revel in it!
5. Be generous. Use lots of physical rewards and be joyous in your praise when working your puppy through their fear. Give lots of food. Make sure your praise is real and motivating. Dogs know when we are fake or insincere.
6. Lead by example. If you are afraid of someone or something, your pup is going to pick up on that! You need to walk with confidence and be self-assured in order to expect the same behavior from your pup.
7. Use the power of the pack. Dogs learn best from other dogs. If you have or know good, balanced dogs that you can use to help build your puppy's confidence, take

advantage of it. When your puppy is able to follow the lead of another dog and conquer their fears, it is a game-changer. I am blessed to have a pack that is confident and unafraid—they are bombproof—and every puppy I raise emulates them. Gunfire? No big deal. Fireworks? Who cares. Going to a parade downtown with thousands of people, hundreds of dogs, kids, chaos, and noise? *No problema.* The power of the pack. It is a thing of beauty!

CONTINUING SOCIALIZATION

Once Phase 3 is over, you should not stop socializing your pup! Consider all seven categories: people, places, sights, sounds, surfaces, animals, and experiences.

What are your puppy's strengths? Continue those with an emphasis on neutral socialization (no rewards). What are their weaknesses? Continue those but use lots of positive socialization (rewards). Your goal is to raise a confident, social, bombproof pup.

The socialization window is open until your puppy is twelve months old. Do not stop now! Keep doing what you are doing.

Chapter Summary

Your puppy is only young once. Socializing your puppy is something you *get* to do. Enjoy it! There is a lot to cover, but if you break it up into the three phases I have given you, it will not feel so overwhelming. Plan ahead. Front-load your puppy's training and you will see it pay dividends in no time.

10. PHYSICAL EXERCISE

"A tired dog is a good dog."
—Every dog trainer!

To be their best selves, dogs need The Big Three: physical exercise, mental stimulation, and training.

This chapter focuses on physical exercise. I give you eleven ways to safely exercise your puppy. These activities are easy to do and fun for both of you. Use them to create an even deeper bond with your four-legged friend.

Enjoy!

SAFETY CONSIDERATIONS

Safety first. Before you start exercising your puppy—beyond the walks and little exercises you have done up to this point—let's discuss a few key safety considerations. Knowing this information will help keep your puppy safe and injury-free so they can live a long, happy, healthy life.

Let's talk about something most owners do not think about: joint health.

JOINT HEALTH

Your puppy's joints are living tissue that grow according to the stresses that are put on them. The right amount of stress helps joints grow strong. Too much stress weakens joints and can lead to injuries and early-onset osteoarthritis.

Your puppy has growth plates in the active new bone areas near the end of the long bones in their limbs. These growth plates are made of cartilage, a rubbery and flexible material. Each long bone has two or more growth plates that control the future shape and length of the mature bone. Growth plates are open and vulnerable to injury until they are done growing, which is typically between twelve and eighteen months of age.

GROWTH PLATE INJURIES

Growth plates are the weakest area of a puppy's growing skeleton, even weaker than the ligaments and tendons connecting their bones to other bones and muscles. For this reason, joint injuries often result in growth plate injuries.

The good news is, growth plates usually heal well. The bad news is, injured growth plates can close prematurely, causing the affected bone to grow unevenly and become deformed.

How do growth plate injuries happen? They are usually the result of falls, twists, collisions, and hard hits. Fast-moving activities and too much repetition can also cause growth plate injuries. It may be funny to watch your puppy slip and slide across hardwood floors or jump off the couch, but these activities can increase the risk of growth plate injuries.

PREVENTING GROWTH PLATE INJURIES

Does this mean you should avoid letting your puppy exercise? No, not at all. Not allowing your puppy to exercise could prevent their joints from reaching their true potential, which means your puppy would not develop a strong skeleton.

The goal is to give your puppy *good* exercise. The best exercise for puppies includes playing with other puppies and dogs of similar energy levels, self-directed play, and short walks that lengthen over time. As your puppy grows, you can gradually introduce activities like stairs, jumping, and swimming.

Avoid too much exercise, excessive bouts of exercise, and singularly overloaded events.

THE GOLDEN RULE

How much exercise is the right amount? The Golden Rule I follow is that a puppy can have five minutes of exercise per month of age, twice a day. For example, an eight-week-old puppy can play twice a day for ten minutes at a time. A four-month-old puppy can play twice a day for twenty minutes at a time.

LOW IMPACT IS BEST

Low-impact exercise is movement that occurs in the body without slamming, jumping, or jarring. It has little to no impact on the joints and gets the heart rate up slowly. The best low-impact exercise for puppies is walking because it is safe on their joints.

ALLOW YOUR PUPPY TO SELF-REGULATE

Puppies will self-regulate, but only if they are given the opportunity to do so. If your puppy is leashed to you for a walk, they will not be able to stop when they are tired. This is why I prefer off-leash exercise for puppies. It allows them to stop when they need to take a break.

Puppies who have a good working relationship with their owner stay close by. If you are worried your puppy might run off, use a harness and long line preventatively.

SURFACE TYPE

Surface type is an important consideration because a puppy's joints are susceptible to injury, and you want to ensure that your puppy is playing and exercising on flat, soft, non-slippery surfaces like carpet, gravel, turf, and grass. Avoid uneven surfaces, hilly areas, slick floors, and concrete.

ENTERING AND EXITING VEHICLES

Until your puppy is about eighteen months old, it is best to help them get in and out of vehicles. *Just because they can does not mean they should.* I always lift puppies in and out of vehicles. As they get older, I let them start hopping in and out, with my assistance, to minimize impact. This helps to prevent injury while also giving them a *can-do* attitude.

OTHER SAFETY CONSIDERATIONS

Beyond joint injuries, there are a few other safety factors at play when exercising your puppy.

OVERHEATING

Dogs do not sweat like humans do. Their primary cooling mechanism is panting. A sign that your pup is too hot and is unable to cool themselves down is when their tongue hangs out of the side of their mouth or ladles and curls upwards.

Exercising in heat, especially when excited, can cause your puppy to overheat quickly. For this reason, it is best to exercise your puppy in the early-morning and late-evening hours during the hot summer months.

Normal body temperature for a dog is 101.0 to 102.5 degrees Fahrenheit. It is a good idea to keep a digital dog thermometer on hand and accessible in case you are ever worried your pup has overheated.

If you need to cool your pup off quickly, put cool water on their chest, belly, and paws (not their head), or make them an ice bath.

BLOAT

Gastric dilatation and volvulus (GDV), also called bloat, occurs when a dog's stomach twists and fills with gas. It is considered one of the most painful, severe emergencies in veterinary medicine. If you have a dog, and especially if you have a deep-chested dog like a Great Dane, Doberman, or German shepherd, you need to know about bloat because it can be deadly.

To help prevent bloat in dogs, it is important to avoid physical activity with your dog one hour before they eat a meal and two hours after.

It is also a good idea to only let your pup drink a small amount of water immediately after exercising. I count to two, tell my puppy "*That's enough*," and then remove them from the water bowl. Eventually they learn to self-regulate.

Once your pup has stopped panting, they can have more water. We will touch on bloat again in Chapter 13.

THE THREE RULES OF PLAY

When it comes to toy play, I have three simple rules for puppies.

These rules keep me safe and make play more enjoyable for both of us.

1. Wait for permission to engage the toy. (Do not jump for it or try to take it from me.)
2. Bring the toy back to me. (Do not run away with it.)
3. Drop the toy on command. (Do not fight me for it.)

Initially, your puppy is not going to know any of these rules, but over time, with play and practice, you will begin teaching them the rules.

Next, let's discuss some fun physical exercise activities you can do with your puppy!

PHYSICAL EXERCISE FOR PUPPIES

When it comes to puppies and exercise, I am sharing my ten favorite things with you! These exercises are listed in order from lowest impact to highest impact (generally speaking). Try one each day and see what your puppy enjoys doing the most!

1. *Pack Walks*

Walking is truly my favorite form of exercise for puppies. It builds a bond between you and your puppy, allows your puppy to self-regulate, is low impact, and leaves your puppy feeling mentally and physically satisfied.

Off-leash pack walks are best. I keep an eye on my puppy, but for the most part I just let her be a dog. I do not call her or expect her to walk next to me. If she is getting into something, digging where she should not, annoying another dog, or drinking yucky water, I intervene. Other than that, I leave her be!

If an off-leash walk is not an option, then use your puppy's long line and harness. Try to keep the leash loose so your puppy is not practicing pulling and learning bad habits. Make sure if your puppy is on a leash (or long line), they learn to follow your lead and go where you go. Never follow your puppy around or allow them to lead you on a walk. You are the leader, not the follower!

I usually take puppies for two walks a day—one in the morning and one in the evening. Short walks are called potty walks. Longer walks are pack walks.

2. *Outside Time*

There is nothing better than fresh air and sunshine, am I right? I swear the happiest dogs are dogs who get to spend most of their day outside, as nature intended.

I love being outside and I enjoy letting puppies hang out with me when I am outside playing with my daughter, pulling weeds, reading books, and working in the garage. Let your puppy be a part of your everyday life; it will help them settle in faster and acclimate more quickly to your home and family.

Even when you don't go for a walk, being outside is mentally stimulating for your puppy and will tire them out quickly. But when your puppy is outside with you, keep an eye on them. Make sure they are behaving themselves. Do not let them do anything now as a puppy that you will not want them doing later as an adult. This includes digging, chasing wildlife, and barking unnecessarily.

If you have mature, well-behaved adult dogs, let them serve as role models for your puppy. Just make sure they are respecting the others' space and not harassing them constantly. Outside time does not always equal playtime. It is important for dogs to simply *exist* together. Pack walks help strengthen this mentality. Play is nice, but there is a time and a place for everything.

Generally, dogs should play less than 10 percent of the time that they are together.

3. *Walking on the Treadmill*

Teaching your puppy to walk on the treadmill is a good confidence builder and a great workout alternative for bad weather days and days when you are busy. Start with short walks, then add more time as your puppy gets older. When your dog is fully mature, you can do longer workouts with changes in pace and incline.

4. *FitPaws*

FitPaws for dogs is like gym equipment for humans. It is a collection of different objects that are designed specifically for dogs and their needs. It provides a physical workout while targeting specific muscle groups, strengthening the core, and helping to prevent injury during other forms of exercise.

I love FitPaws (and similar) products. For puppies, I primarily use it as a confidence builder. Once they are older, I use it for body awareness, individual limb awareness, and strength and conditioning training. FitPaws is ideal for draining both physical and mental energy.

5. *Swimming*

Swimming is an excellent low-impact workout. Puppies cannot swim for very long or very far, but it tires them out quickly!

When introduced correctly, swimming can be one of your puppy's favorite summertime workouts to beat the heat! I highly recommend a doggie life jacket for when your puppy is older and swimming longer distances though. Safety first!

6. *Playing with Other Dogs*

Dog-to-dog play is a great physical workout. It sharpens social skills, provides an all-body workout, and teaches bite inhibition.

Puppy play is such an important part of puppy raising that I dedicate an entire chapter to it. Check out Chapter 12 to learn more about puppy play.

7. *Agility*

Dog agility is a sport where you direct your dog through a series of obstacles on a course within a set period of time. While puppies are much too young to compete in agility themselves, it is perfectly acceptable to introduce your puppy to the sport of agility and try basic (low, small) obstacles to help your puppy get the hang of things. Pick easy obstacles and use lots of food (or treats) and praise as rewards.

If you do not have agility equipment or do not have access to it, try DIY agility where you make obstacles at home with items you have in the house or garage. You will be amazed at how much fun it is to be creative. Even something as simple as a ladder can make for a great agility obstacle. Lay it flat and have your puppy step through the rungs. The options are endless!

Urban agility, also called dog parkour, is a canine version of getting your dog on, in, and around various obstacles. It is a great confidence builder and is very physically and mentally tiring.

My favorite place to do urban agility is public playgrounds. It is a great way to socialize your puppy with kids while building their confidence in new places and on new surfaces.

8. *Tug*

Tug play taps into a dog's deeply rooted genetic instincts to chase, pounce, bite, and shake prey. It teaches impulse control, builds confidence, and serves as a great way to bond with your new puppy.

Do not worry about the nitty-gritty mechanics of tug play—like bite development, targeting, gripping, and outing—instead, introduce your puppy to tug play so that you can start having fun with it.

If your puppy is not interested in playing tug, try again later when they are closer to a year old. You might see an uptick in interest due to age and maturity. (Prey drive generally increases with age.)

9. Fetch

Can I be honest with you? Fetch is one of my *least* favorite exercises for dogs. It winds them up and leaves them physically tired but mentally wired. It also creates a lot of conflict for naturally possessive dogs who do not always want to follow The Three Rules of Play.

There is a time and a place for everything, though, so fetch is not blacklisted. It just should not be a primary activity for your dog. Once a week is fine, but no more than that.

Fetch can be hard on puppy joints as well, because it involves a lot of running, jumping, and twisting. If you have an intense and very driven puppy, I recommend waiting until they are older and better trained before playing fetch.

10. Flirt Pole

Like I mentioned back in Chapter 2, a flirt pole is a long pole made of a light yet sturdy material. It has a long string or rope attached to one end and a lure (like a toy) fastened to the other. It closely resembles a fishing pole—minus the hook, of course.

Flirt poles are a great way to give your puppy physical exercise while teaching coordination. You are able to control the flirt pole's movements and keep your puppy close to you while playing. It is fun for humans and pups alike!

Playing with a flirt pole should be done on a soft surface. Play for only a few minutes at a time to minimize joint stress. Keep the slip lead on your puppy so that they stay with you and do not try to run away with their prize!

A FEW WORDS ON EXERCISE

I want to mention that exercise involving toys and play, like fetch and playdates with other dogs, is going to wind your puppy up. This exercise is fun, but it should be done in moderation (only two to three times per week).

On the flip side, exercise involving slow, continuous movement, like walks and exploring outside, is going to calm your puppy down, help them relax and decompress, and tire them out. This exercise, overall, is healthier for your puppy and should constitute the bulk of the exercise that you do with them.

Additionally, if you have a working dog, or if your puppy was bred for a specific job, I would encourage you to look for opportunities to explore those activities in your local area. If you have a border collie, for example, is there anyone nearby who offers herding lessons? If you have a terrier, is there any barn hunting? What about agility, rally obedience competitions, protection sport "IGP" training, or dock diving?

Allowing your dog to exercise in a way that fulfills their genetic propensity for a particular activity is the best way to satisfy them. German shepherds and Australian shepherds, for example, are highly versatile dogs who excel in multiple venues. I do agility, bite work, dock diving, herding, lure coursing, nosework, rally, and various other sports and activities with my dogs. It gives them a very fulfilling and satisfying life while keeping things fun and fresh for us!

Happy cattle dog puppy herding sheep at Valor K9 Academy—Spokane, circa 2015.

CHAPTER SUMMARY

I have just given you eleven fun and exciting ways to tire out your puppy, as well as ideas for other sports and activities. Get out there and find activities you both enjoy!

Exercise is an important part of a balanced, healthy lifestyle for puppies. Try to meet your puppy's physical exercise needs five to six days each week—not seven. A day or two off is important for your pup's physical and mental well-being.

11.

MENTAL STIMULATION

"Dogs need mental stimulation. It gives them a job to do."

—Amy Pishner

Have you ever sat in a long lecture and at the end you walked out feeling exhausted and ready for a nap? You had not done anything physical yet you were tired. Why? Because the lecture was mentally stimulating. You were thinking, processing information, and problem-solving, all of which take energy and brain power.

All living beings have two types of energy. We have physical energy that requires physical exercise, and we have mental energy that requires mental exercise. Mental exercise is also called *mental stimulation*. It is *número dos* in The Big Three.

Mental stimulation is exercise for the mind and involves challenging your dog's intelligence, teaching them new things, and letting them problem-solve to come up with solutions on their own.

A lot of what you have already done has provided your puppy with mental stimulation. Activities like obedience training, socialization, tethered decompression, and exercise are all mentally stimulating.

In this chapter, I teach you how to dynamically target your puppy's brain power by challenging them with new forms of mental stimulation.

MENTAL STIMULATION FOR PUPPIES

I am going to give you six new ways to provide your puppy with mental stimulation. These activities are fun, challenging, and perfect for bad weather or days when you are tired or busier than usual. These activities only take a few minutes to do and are tremendously effective at draining your puppy's mental energy reserves.

A FEW REMINDERS FIRST...

- Keep your sessions short and sweet.
- Start and end on a good note to leave your puppy wanting more.
- Use a good motivator. I usually use kibble, but sometimes I switch to high-value treats.
- Make sure your praise is enthusiastic.
- Have fun! Your puppy's energy level will reflect yours.

Are you ready to jump right in?

Here are six mental stimulation activities for your puppy.

1. NOSEWORK

Nosework is an activity that allows your dog to fulfill their natural desire to hunt. It harnesses their unique scenting abilities and uses plenty of brainpower in the process. Nosework is three times more tiring than other mentally stimulating activities. Sniff, sniff, sniff!

There is a formal sport called K9 Nose Work, but the nosework I like to do with puppies is very informal. It teaches them to use their nose, which builds confidence and reinforces overall stability. It also helps them track down items of interest, like kibble and treats.

Introducing nosework is fun and easy! You can start by holding your puppy back and allowing them to watch you hide food along one or two walls in a room. Bring them back to the first "hide" in the room and tell them "*Find it*!" With the leash attached to the harness, follow them as they hunt for each piece of food. Using their nose is tiring. When they find all the pieces, praise them and tell them "All done," or do another hide in another part of the room. Start with easy hides, then work toward progressively harder hides.

Always end on a good note and when they still want to do more!

2. CLICKER TRAINING

Next up is clicker training! The clicker is a device that gives a consistent sound (called a "click") and is conditioned with a reward, like a piece of kibble or a treat. The click is non-emotional and hits a different part of your puppy's brain than a verbal marker does. It communicates to your puppy that when they hear the click, whatever behavior they were doing in that moment will produce a reward. Clicking is like taking a mental photograph of your puppy's behavior, which encourages them to offer that same behavior, or a similar behavior, again.

I like to use the clicker for two purposes: tricks training and free shaping, where you allow the dog to creatively come up with behaviors to meet your objective. Before you can do either of those, you need to start by conditioning the clicker for your puppy. I call this "*clicker charging*." It is simple and easy.

To charge the clicker, simply compress the clicker (*click*!), then pause for one to two seconds, and reward your dog with a piece of food.

It will take about 120 to 150 repetitions to condition the clicker for your puppy. This means if you do one-minute sessions with about twelve to fifteen clicks per session, you are looking at approximately ten sessions of clicker charging before you are ready to actually use the clicker for tricks training and free shaping.

Once the clicker is charged, you can start using it!

Tricks

Tricks are cute behaviors your dog can learn simply for the sake of amusement. Some popular tricks include "Shake," "Sit pretty," and "Roll over." Most tricks can be taught using one of the three core techniques: luring, capturing, or shaping. When you're teaching a trick, stick to that one trick until the behavior is complete and *don't name it 'til you love it*! This means you should not start calling the trick by its name (for example, "Shake") until after your dog is easily lifting their paw when you reach out your hand.

When your puppy knows a series of tricks, they will generally "offer" the trick they learned first, the one they are rewarded for the most, or the one they learned most recently. Choose wisely! I generally wait until later to teach tricks like "Shake" and "Speak" because those are undesirable behaviors otherwise. I like teaching calm tricks like "Pout" or "Play dead."

Free Shaping

Free shaping teaches your dog to learn from their *own* behavior and to offer new behaviors in the process. There are two ways to free shape. One involves coming up with a behavior and then clicking *successively* as your dog offers behaviors that are closer and closer to that end goal. The other involves clicking each time your dog offers a new behavior. Both are super beneficial and challenging!

When introducing puppies to free shaping, it usually takes one to two sessions for them to get the hang of things. This is completely normal and will probably be the case for your puppy. Why? Because, up until this point, your puppy has been trained to look at you for information and cues regarding what you want them to do. Free shaping takes your puppy's thinking in the complete opposite direction by giving them the freedom to offer any behavior they want to. The clicker then reinforces behaviors you want, and your puppy learns from their own actions. Once they catch on, it is very rewarding to see the wheels start turning!

Free shaping is an enjoyable way to exercise your puppy's mind and teach them a new way of thinking. It is especially useful for handler-dependent dogs or dogs who lack confidence.

3. STUFFED KONGS

We all need a cheat day sometimes, right? A stuffed KONG is one of the easiest ways to provide your dog with mental stimulation. It satisfies their chewing and foraging instincts while exercising their mind.

A KONG is a durable, non-toxic, rubber dog toy with a hollow center and two holes. It can be stuffed with food and given to your puppy right away or it can be stuffed with food and some frozen liquid and given to your dog later on for an added challenge.

Make sure the KONG you buy is larger than your dog's trachea, and upsize as your puppy grows. I use a large KONG for all the dogs in my household, including puppies.

My favorite KONG recipe is very simple:

- peanut butter
- coconut oil
- chia seeds
- bananas
- kibble

Another recipe I like is:

- canned dog food
- pumpkin
- yogurt
- blueberries
- dehydrated beef liver

My dogs do not get stuffed KONGs often, but they sure love it when they do. It is a special treat!

Need inspiration? Check out other great recipes online!

4. INTERACTIVE TOYS

Interactive toys are in the same grouping as stuffed KONGs except you do not freeze them. Interactive toys are brain games for dogs and require more thinking and problem-solving than stuffed KONGs. You hide food in the toys, and the dog works to get the food out.

My two favorite interactive toys are the KONG Wobbler and the Starmark Treat Dispensing Chewball. There is a plethora of interactive toys out there. Pick whatever makes your heart happy! I have just a few interactive toys for my dogs because in my household, less is more.

When first using interactive toys, you might fill them with a combination of kibble and treats to make them more appealing to your puppy. If your puppy is super food-motivated, kibble alone works just fine.

5. TETHERED DECOMPRESSION

Per Chapter 8 (Obedience Training), tethered decompression (TD) is a great mental stimulation activity. It is easy for you to do and involves very little effort on your part. TD is best to do after physical activity and training so that your puppy is tired and calm. I like doing TD in the evenings for twenty to sixty minutes at a time while I cook, clean, or watch television.

Tethered decompression allows your puppy to be a part of the family without getting underfoot and habituates them to everyday life.

6. FOOD THROWS

The last cheat-day option I am going to leave you with is what I call "food throws." This is, quite simply, where you take a handful of food and toss it outside and allow your dog to forage for it. You can throw food on the turf like I do or you can throw food in grass. Do not throw it into gravel or sand, though, because you do not want your dog to ingest them. Ingesting sand especially can lead to sand impaction, which can be deadly.

Food throws are a simple way to give your dog their food with little effort on your part. I enjoy doing food throws with my entire pack. They are respectful and do not fight over food. It is enjoyable for everyone!

Chapter Summary

As you can see, mental stimulation is a lot of fun! Find what you both enjoy doing the most and do that! I like to do some sort of mental stimulation every day with my dogs. It is easy to do, only takes a few minutes, and has tremendous benefits for their mental exercise needs.

When you combine physical exercise with mental stimulation and training—The Big Three—the result is a tired, happy, fulfilled dog who has a great quality of life.

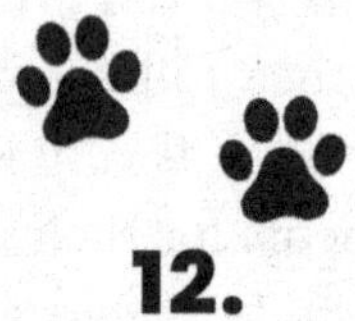

12.

PUPPY PLAY

"For a dog, emotion is displayed through body language, while intention is displayed through motion."

—Cesar Milan

This is an information-packed chapter that you are going to love. I teach you the ins and outs of proper puppy play, including lining up playdates, supervising play, and knowing when to step in versus when to let puppies figure things out themselves.

In this chapter, this topic starts with owner education, and, in the online puppy course, it ends with me narrating live play sessions so that owners can witness proper puppy play for themselves and learn from it.

My goal is to educate you so that you can set your puppy up for success and raise a confident, well-socialized dog.

Be sure to read this entire chapter before taking your sweet puppy on their first playdate!

OWNER EDUCATION

CANINE BODY LANGUAGE

Learning to read canine body language is critical. It can be the difference between a *great* play session and a terrible one. Your puppy communicates with their body, so learning to "read" what they are saying is tremendously powerful. It allows you to connect with your puppy and advocate for them on a whole new level.

You do not need to be a body language expert to learn to read your puppy, but you do need to understand some basics to have a general idea of how they are doing during a play session. The goal is for your puppy to be comfortable, not overwhelmed, while having a good overall time playing with other dogs.

Learning to read body language will help you to better assess your puppy's feelings before, during, and after play.

Here is what you need to pay attention to.

THE FIVE KEY AREAS OF BODY LANGUAGE

1. HEAD

First, look at your puppy's head. The head tells you a lot about what a dog is thinking and feeling.

Are they carrying it high and proud? Are they looking around excitedly and making solid eye contact? Are their eyes soft or excited and full of mischief? Are they blinking normally? Is their mouth open and relaxed? Are they breathing normally or a little faster than usual? Are their ears forward and alert?

These are signs of a comfortable albeit excited puppy.

Or is your puppy's head held low? Are they ducking down? Are they averting their gaze or looking away? Are they avoiding eye contact? Does their face appear frozen? Are they furrowing their brow or pinning their ears? Is their mouth shut, or are they panting heavily?

These are signs of a nervous, uncomfortable puppy.

2. TAIL

Next, look at the tail. A confident puppy wags their tail high and proud. It goes back and forth, at a normal speed or very quickly, to show that they are excited and engaged.

A nervous puppy's tail wags low and slow. When they are afraid, their tail tucks under their butt and touches their belly. These are signs that they are uncomfortable.

3. HACKLES

When the hair on your dog's back stands up, it is called *"hackles."* Observe your puppy's hackles carefully. They are a key piece of information that tells us what our dogs are feeling.

When a dog's hackles are up, it means they are feeling an adrenaline rush. It does not necessarily mean they are aggressive. It can also be a sign of nervousness, excitement, or dominance.

It is normal for a puppy's hackles to sometimes go up when meeting another dog, especially if they have not been socialized much yet or are meeting a new dog for the first time. It is normal for them to feel adrenalized, but, if the play session is going well, then the adrenaline rush should subside and the hackles should go down.

The goal is to have a well-socialized puppy who does not get an adrenaline rush when meeting or playing with other dogs. If your puppy does continue to put their hackles up, do not fret. You may have a more excitable, less confident, or more dominant dog.

If you socialize your puppy properly, their hackles should come down more quickly with each successive playdate.

4. POSTURE

Posture says a lot about a dog's comfort level and confidence. A confident puppy stands tall with their head held high and their weight evenly distributed on all four paws. They step lightly, have relaxed and fluid movement, and are never stiff or rigid.

A nervous puppy slouches with their head hung low and their weight primarily over their back feet. They hide behind their owner, snap at other dogs, and try to avoid physical contact. A nervous or nervous-submissive dog may lay down and expose their belly to another dog or pee when another dog approaches. They are tense and trying to communicate their discomfort with the current situation.

5. VOCALIZATIONS

Vocalizations are the noises you hear from your puppy. They are the final clue about how your puppy is feeling and what they are thinking. How your puppy *sounds* is a good indicator of how they feel.

A confident puppy yips, barks, and whines excitedly. Their vocalizations are rapid and high-pitched, indicating a playful and enthusiastic state of mind.

A nervous puppy growls, yelps, snaps, and/or bites at other dogs while hiding behind you, ducking, or running for cover. Their vocalizations are deep and low or high and screechy, both of which indicate fear and discomfort. Oftentimes, when a puppy is overwhelmed, they will yelp and run for cover. This means the dog they are playing with is too dominant or overbearing for them.

Sometimes when dogs play, they vocalize, and that is okay as long as the vocalizations point to excitement and not fear. Usually, once puppies settle in and learn each other's play style, they find common ground and tend to be less vocal during play.

The most common vocalization to hear during play is growling. As long as both puppies are growling and the play appears to be going well, do not worry about it. It is normal for some puppies to vocalize at times during play. They are having fun.

LITTER TYPE

Next, let's talk about doggie temperament types. Within a litter of puppies, there are three overarching temperament types: alpha, middle, and back. Knowing which litter type your puppy is will help you arrange suitable playdates. It is good information to have, but sometimes you learn through trial and error about who your puppy plays best with.

ALPHA

Alpha dogs are the minority. Approximately 10 percent of dogs or less are true alpha dogs. They are naturally extremely confident, dominant, assertive, and fearless. They walk into the room like they own it. When alpha dogs reach maturity, they generally do not get along with other alpha dogs, and there is nothing wrong with that. It is natural—as nature intended. Alpha dogs can be both male and female.

MIDDLE

Middle dogs are the majority. About 80 percent of dogs are middle dogs. Some middle dogs are dominant by default if they lack human leadership. They play the role of alpha with both their human and canine pack members, which is problematic. Other middle dogs are laid-back, happy-go-lucky, and easy to get along with. Middle dogs usually thrive in social settings as long as they have been properly socialized. Statistically speaking, your dog is probably a middle dog.

BACK

Back dogs make up the final 10 percent of dogs. They are naturally very submissive dogs who avoid conflict, get along well with alpha dogs, and can sometimes be the subject of bullying by dominant-by-default middle dogs. Back dogs are *usually* the dogs who roll on their backs and pee when meeting a new dog. They make it very clear to the other dog that they are not a threat and do not wish to challenge anyone.

MY PERSONAL DOGS

My male German shepherd, Havok, is an alpha dog. He is a born leader and the overseer of our pack. He is calm, confident, and assertive. Other dogs recognize his authority and go out of their way to submit to him. As a mature dog, he plays with Zoey and a few select temporary pack members but never with other alpha males. He is extremely tolerant and not easily provoked. He is easy to handle and very biddable, thanks to great genetics and early training.

My female Australian shepherd, Zoey, is a middle dog. She is incredibly balanced and neutral around dogs. She prefers playing with male dogs but will play with females too.

Both of my dogs deflect to me as their pack leader. They are well socialized, neutral in social settings, and playful when the time is right. Together, they are the alpha and beta of my pack, and they absolutely love each other. They have been instrumental in helping me raise, train, and rehabilitate thousands of dogs over the years.

I am extremely grateful for them.

WHICH TEMPERAMENT TYPE IS YOUR DOG?

Knowing which temperament type your dog is can be super helpful when it comes to picking playmates. Alpha dogs do not usually get along with other alpha dogs. Dominant-by-default middle dogs should not be paired with back dogs. Laid-back middle dogs get along with everyone. Back dogs prefer dogs that are easy-going and gentle during play.

You may not know your dog's temperament type until you schedule a few playdates. Observe your dog during play and pay close attention to their body language and play style, which I discuss next.

PLAY STYLES

When dogs play, it is as if they are striking up a conversation with each other. Initially, the conversation might be slow and awkward or it might be fast-paced and overwhelming. If you are lucky, they hit it off right away and play like they have been friends forever.

A dog's play style usually matches their energy level. High-energy dogs have a fast, rough-and-tumble play style that involves lots of running and chasing. Low-energy dogs take things slow.

A high-energy dog is too much dog for a low-energy dog. Medium-energy dogs play best together. Usually, the more closely you can match energy, the better the play session goes.

HEALTHY PLAY

What does healthy play look like, you ask? It involves several different components.

1. HEALTHY PLAY INVOLVES ROLE REVERSAL.

What this means is that during play, the dog on top switches to become the dog on the bottom. The dog doing the chasing allows themselves to become the one being chased. Role reversal is an important part of healthy play. It allows play to be mutual and mutually enjoyable.

2. HEALTHY PLAY INVOLVES PLAY PAUSES.

A play pause is when two dogs break away from play to catch their breath for a few seconds, plop down, or sniff around a little. Play pauses naturally slow down the pace of play. Dogs who naturally take play pauses understand the importance of them and have a better sense of healthy play habits. Many puppies do not take play pauses unless you make them, so make them!

To teach puppies to take a play pause, simply catch them, leash them up, and separate them from each other for a few minutes. When they resume play, it *should* be at a slower pace than before. Puppies who are amped up should be required to take breaks often via play pauses.

3. HEALTHY PLAY IS HORIZONTAL.

Healthy play is horizontal. It involves running, keeping all four paws on the ground, and laying down during play. Unhealthy play is vertical. Dogs stand up on their back legs and appear to be sparring. Vertical play is usually dominance-based and can lead to a fight. Vertical play should be stopped right away and the dogs should be separated until they settle down. If vertical play continues, the dogs are simply not a good match for each other. They are too dominant by nature to play nicely together.

4. HEALTHY PLAY INCLUDES PLAY BOWS.

A play bow is when a dog puts their front paws on the ground and their butt in the air, like they are bowing. Play bows are a dog's way of saying, "*Hey! Come play with me*!" They are an invitation to play, and when met by a dog who's also interested in playing, play bows usually lead to play. They are a great thing to see and can happen any time before or during play. When a dog play bows during a play session, it means, "*Yep! We're still playing here*!" It is a form of communication.

5. HEALTHY PLAY DOES NOT ESCALATE.

When play escalates and gets faster, louder, or more vertical, it means the dogs are not learning to match each other's play style and a fight is on the horizon. Escalating play can also signal bullying, where one dog is constantly forcing the other dog to play, despite the dog's objections, and the play is not mutual or mutually enjoyable. Play that escalates should be stopped immediately and a play pause should be enacted.

6. HEALTHY PLAY INCLUDES SELF-HANDICAPPING.

Self-handicapping is where the bigger or more dominant dog handicaps themselves by laying down or rolling onto their back during play. This behavior allows the smaller or less dominant dog to feel like an equal and to have the upper hand at times during play. A well-balanced adult dog self-handicaps often during play with puppies. This builds the puppy's confidence and allows them to enjoy playing with larger, more capable dogs.

7. HEALTHY PLAY IS MOSTLY QUIET.

By and large, healthy play is quiet or includes only soft, quiet growling. There are exceptions, however, as some dogs are vocal in general and like to bark during play. These are also usually higher-energy dogs who have a more high-speed play style. For dogs who have found common ground, their play is usually rather quiet.

UNHEALTHY PLAY

Signs of Unhealthy Play:

- No role reversals
- One dog is always on top or always doing the chasing
- No play pauses
- Play is constant and/or escalating
- Play is vertical where the front paws are off the ground and the dogs are standing on their back legs
- Play is continuously escalating and getting faster and more intense
- No self-handicapping; instead, the bigger and more dominant dog stays in the dominant position
- Dogs get louder and louder with constant growling from one or both dogs

Unhealthy play can lead to a fight and should be stopped right away.

OTHER PLAY CONSIDERATIONS

A ONE-TO-ONE RATIO

When setting up a playdate, it is best to let your puppy play with just one new puppy at a time. Remember, puppies learning to play together are striking up a conversation. This is best done in a one-on-one setting. When three or more puppies are involved in play, it can become overwhelming for those who are still learning to communicate with their fellow canines, which can lead to overstimulation and misunderstandings.

There is nothing wrong with larger groups of puppies playing, but these play sessions must be supervised by attentive owners or trainers who can read each puppy's body language in an instant.

The goal is for your puppy to have positive play experiences to set them up for success in the years to come.

PLAY SURFACE

Puppy play is best done outside on a soft surface. I prefer to use turf grass or a fenced-in yard for puppy play. This allows the puppies to play in a safe, supervised area that is easy on their joints.

PLAY LOCATION

Do *not* take your puppy to dog parks or doggie daycare for socialization. These places are not safe places for your puppy to socialize with other dogs. They are not intimate settings. They are like mosh pits for dogs, where wild, uncontrolled behavior runs rampant. They are also breeding grounds for diseases like parvo.

PLAY DURATION

Puppy playdates should be short and sweet, no more than ten to fifteen minutes. Always try to end on a good note, when the puppies are still having fun and before they get overwhelmed, overstimulated, or overtired. Puppies are much like toddlers in that sense!

INTRODUCING DOGS

The best way to introduce your puppy to another dog is to start with both dogs on leash. Stand about five feet apart. Wait for them to settle down and lower their energy. When both dogs are calm, tell your puppy to "Go say hi," then step towards the other dog. This signals to your puppy that it is okay to greet the other dog.

While the dogs meet, try to keep the leashes from tangling. This will help you pull back your puppy in case the meeting goes south.

Generally, when puppies meet, they are going to take turns sniffing each other's butts (I call this a "doggie handshake") and then walk away from each other or play together. Puppies rarely fight; usually, if anything, one puppy is too shy to play and tries to avoid the other one. In this case, step back with the more confident puppy and give the shy puppy some time to warm up.

If you are in a safe, secure location and your puppy is playing nicely with the other dog, you can unclip the leashes.

If you are introducing your puppy to an adult dog, allow your puppy to step towards the adult dog, not the other way around. Do not allow the adult dog to approach your puppy. Ask the owner of the adult dog to stay in one spot with their dog so your puppy can approach on their own terms. This sets the stage for building confidence and keeps your puppy from feeling overwhelmed during the initial meeting.

NARRATING PLAY

To watch me narrate live play sessions with Stella, my Puppy Head Start student in the course, feel free to check out the videos available on my website at www.valork9academyonline.com or scan the QR codes below.

Puppy Play Video 1:

Puppy Play Video 2

Chapter Summary

Understanding canine body language and puppy play is a critical component of responsible pet ownership and advocacy. Dogs talk, but only to those who listen!

13.

HEALTH AND WELLNESS

"The optimal approach to training is a holistic one."

—Amy Pishner

Physical and mental exercises are not the only factors that impact your dog's health and wellness. Most dog owners do not realize how much a dog's diet impacts their behavior. Just like in humans, poor-quality food—especially kibble filled with fillers, artificial dyes, and low-grade ingredients—can lead to hyperactivity, irritability, anxiety, and difficulty focusing. Dogs fed a "junk food" diet often experience energy spikes and crashes, making training and calm behavior much harder to achieve. A healthy gut is directly linked to better mood and emotional regulation, so feeding high-quality, nutrient-dense food supports both physical and behavioral wellness. Simply put: you cannot expect good behavior from a dog fueled by bad food.

This chapter covers food and goes beyond nutrition to cover other important topics like weight management, grooming, and medical considerations for long-term health. My goal is to point you in the right direction so that you can do your own independent study and make informed decisions for your dog's well-being.

I want your dog to live a long, happy, healthy life.

NUTRITION

With young puppies, I feed primarily kibble from two to six months of age. This is because I am using food as a reward for training, and kibble is the easiest and most sanitary option for that.

I pick only the best kibble to feed my puppies. As you might remember from Chapter 2, I read labels, look for quality ingredients, avoid by-products and fillers like corn, and focus on kibble that lists protein as its first and second ingredients. I prefer hooved animals, like beef and lamb, and I feed both grain-in and grain-free foods. I like a kibble that is a decent size for training that my puppy can swallow quickly and easily.

Once the puppy is four months old, I begin incorporating raw.

WHAT IS A RAW DIET?

A raw diet for dogs consists of uncooked protein meat, raw crushed (or whole) bones, organs (like liver and kidney), eggs, fruits, vegetables, probiotics, and vitamin supplements.

Wolves in the wild eat a raw diet (well, aside from the probiotic and vitamin supplements). They chase, kill their prey, and eat it on the spot. A raw diet—made of fresh, whole foods—is, without a doubt, better for dogs than kibble.

Kibble is highly processed and cooked at high temperatures, which zaps most of the nutrients out of it. Raw is nutrient-dense and biologically appropriate for carnivores like dogs. Dogs are genetic meat eaters; raw food is the most nutritionally compatible option for them.

Fed is good. Raw is best!

HOW TO INTRODUCE RAW

How do I begin introducing raw, you ask? Around four months of age, you can start offering small amounts of raw food to your puppy on a daily basis. For example, you might give your puppy some ground beef, chicken breast, a few bites of turkey neck, an egg (minus the shell), a carrot, broccoli, or apple slices with a little non-flavored Greek yogurt.

Meat, bones, and organs should be raw and uncooked. Fruits and veggies can be lightly sauteed or steamed.

Introducing your puppy to raw food early on teaches them to try new foods and helps their digestive system learn to handle new foods without digestive upset (diarrhea).

A little here and a little there is key!

ARE BONES DANGEROUS?

You might have heard that bones are dangerous for dogs. *Cooked bones* are dangerous because they can splinter in your dog's stomach, perforating the intestinal walls and causing serious injury or even death.

Raw, uncooked bones are safe for dogs. They are soft, which means they are safe. Your puppy simply needs to learn to chew them as opposed to swallowing them whole. You can do this by holding the bone in your hand while your puppy gnaws on it.

THE END GOAL

The end goal is that by six to eight months of age, your puppy is primarily eating a raw-based diet. My dogs' diet follows my 70/10/10/5/5 raw diet plan. This means I feed approximately 70 percent raw animal protein, 10 percent organ, 10 percent bone, 5 percent fruits and veggies, and 5 percent vitamin supplements.

With older puppies and adult dogs, I still use kibble for training, but dinner is comprised of a raw meal that loosely follows my 70/10/10/5/5 plan. How much I feed is based on their age and adult weight.

Here is a typical raw meal for my adult dogs:

- raw hamburger meat
- beef liver
- chicken quarter
- elk scraps

- turkey neck
- chicken paws
- raw egg with membrane
- broccoli and pineapple sauteed in bone broth
- immunity support vitamin, joint support vitamin, and other supplements

SUPPLEMENTS

Let's talk a little about supplements! When it comes to supplements for puppies, there is a lot to take into consideration. Size and growth are two major factors. The goal is for your puppy to grow slow and grow right. For this reason, I avoid calcium supplements. Too much calcium is not good for puppies and can cause joint problems.

I recommend doing your own research for your dog's breed and size before beginning a supplement regimen. Some supplements you might find that are recommended for your puppy include: vitamin E for coat, skin, and overall health; fish oil for skin, coat, and heart health; vitamin C for joint health and immunity; glucosamine and chondroitin for joint health, and cod liver oil for immunity.

I give my dogs supplements from a company called NuVet Labs. I like their immunity and joint support supplements (green and blue bottles). NuVet Plus includes vitamins A, E, and C, and phosphorous, potassium, zinc, and selenium for immunity. NuVet Joint contains glucosamine, chondroitin, MSM, and vitamin C, which are beneficial for protecting and preserving a dog's joints.

To buy online, you will need a purchase code at checkout. You can use my code: 45459.

THE BENEFITS OF RAW

The benefits of feeding raw include:

- first-hand knowledge of everything your dog is eating
- shinier, healthier skin and coat

- less shedding
- cleaner, whiter teeth
- improved body condition and muscle tone
- smaller and fewer bowel movements

The list goes on and on! Check out raw feeding groups on social media. There is a whole world of raw feeding out there and so much to learn. Dig in!

Feeding raw is one of the best things you can do for your dog.

WHAT ABOUT COST?

It is a common misconception that feeding raw is more expensive than feeding kibble or that feeding raw is unaffordable if you are on a fixed income. This is not necessarily true.

There are two ways to source raw: purchasing it premade, which is expensive, or sourcing it yourself and making your dog's meals at home, which is the more economical option. Premade raw can cost upwards of ten dollars a pound. Sourcing raw yourself generally costs two to five dollars a pound, depending on what you buy and where you source it from. The way I do raw, it costs me around two dollars per pound. This is cheaper than kibble!

FOODS TO AVOID

Some foods are toxic for dogs.

Avoid the following toxic foods:

- alcohol
- apples
- apricots
- cherries
- plum seeds/pits
- avocados
- caffeine and coffee grounds
- large amounts of chocolate

- macadamia nuts, almonds, and pistachios
- milk and dairy products
- wild mushrooms
- nutmeg and cinnamon
- onions, chives, and leeks
- excessive amounts of salt
- spicy foods
- sugar-free peanut butter
- green or unripe tomatoes
- raw potatoes
- tobacco
- yeast and raw dough

HEALTHY LEFTOVERS

If you have healthy leftovers, save them for your puppy. Any time we have unwanted dinner leftovers or I clean out the fridge, I always give the leftovers to my dogs. Do not feed your dog from the table. Instead, save the food for later and put it in your dog's food bowl.

OTHER HEALTHY OPTIONS

If feeding raw is not an option for you, I encourage you to look into other healthy options like freeze-dried food, dehydrated food, and canned food. These are great options for dogs. Unprocessed or less processed food is best.

WEIGHT MANAGEMENT

Fat is not cute. Love your puppy enough to not let them get fat—both now and later as an adult dog. Health equals longevity.

Do not look at the number on the scale.

To determine if your puppy is a healthy weight, look for these three things:

1. *A waist.* From above and looking down at your puppy in a standing position, you should see an indented waist.
2. *The last two ribs.* For short-haired dogs, you should be able to see your puppy's last two ribs. For long-haired dogs, you should be able to *feel* your puppy's last two ribs.
3. *A waist tuck.* From the side, you should see a noticeable tuck in your dog's abdomen.

Oftentimes, veterinarians and other pet professionals cannot identify a healthy weight on a dog. They may say that your pet is a good weight when in fact your pet is overweight. Sometimes they may say your dog is too thin when they are not. Be sure to cross-reference with other pet professionals to seek second and third opinions if someone tells you that your dog is over or underweight.

Lean is good. If you feed your puppy a quality diet rich in animal protein and animal fats and if your puppy is getting age-appropriate exercise, they should be lean and fit. That is the goal!

Eighteen-month-old Valor Protection Dog Freya, circa 2023.

FILLING OUT

Your puppy is going to be lean and gangly (for lack of a better word) until they start to fill out. With maturity comes muscle. Most dogs grow *up* first and reach their adult height at around twelve months of age. Then they grow *out*, bulk up, and put on muscle, reaching their mature adult weight at around four to five years of age.

Let your dog grow slowly. Do not overfeed them in an attempt to make them look bigger. Fat is not good and too much weight on a growing frame stresses the joints. Be careful! You alone are responsible for your dog's health.

PREVENTING DYSPLASIA

If you have a large-breed dog or a dog whose breed is prone to hip or elbow dysplasia, such as German shepherds, Labrador retrievers, golden retrievers, rottweilers, and Great Danes, listen carefully—your dog's propensity for becoming dysplastic is not purely genetic. What I mean is, it is not always the breeder's fault if your dog develops dysplasia. Environmental factors come into play as well.

Feed your dog a quality, raw diet, keep them lean, let them grow slowly, and do not allow them to become fat. Limit high-impact exercise. Allow them to self-regulate during play. Give them plenty of time outside in the sun for vitamin D. Feed them a diet that's high in vitamin C. Lift them in and out of the car and avoid stairs and slick floors whenever possible.

These will all help to prevent dysplasia.

A FINAL WORD ON WEIGHT

Remember, as you are feeding your growing puppy, you want to feed them the amount of food suggested for their *adult* weight, not their current weight. For example, a fifty pound, six-month-old male German shepherd who is expected to be eighty-five pounds at maturity should be eating enough food for their expected adult weight, not their current puppy weight. This is important to ensure your puppy is getting enough food to eat and is not underfed.

Exact feeding guidelines are difficult to predict. It will be based on your puppy's age, breed, energy level, and quality of diet. If you are not sure, ask your veterinarian or the puppy's breeder.

Ultimately, your puppy will decide how much they want to eat, but if they are always hungry, make sure you are giving them quality, nutrient-dense food that is high in animal proteins and fats. When in doubt, consult your veterinarian if you have any concerns regarding your puppy's weight or appetite as there could be an underlying medical issue at hand.

GROOMING

Grooming is an area of pet ownership that is oftentimes overlooked. People rely on their veterinarians to clip their puppy's nails or they let their groomer do all of their dog's brushing or bathing. This is a mistake! As your dog's owner, you should be directly involved in your pet's grooming and maintenance.

You should be able to do basic grooming on your dog. This ensures that they see you as the pack leader and teaches them to be calm and respectful during the grooming process.

Here is what I recommend for grooming.

BATHS

During the potty-training process, you will bathe your puppy any time they have an accident in their crate and get dirty. This can be a mini bath to clean their paws or belly or a full bath if they are covered in pee or poop.

Once your puppy is potty-trained, bathe them only when necessary. The less you wash them, the better. You want their coat to retain its natural oils to help keep it soft and smooth. Too much bathing dries out the coat and can lead to itchiness.

I use Dawn dish soap for puppy baths. For adult dogs, I use Dawn dish soap followed by dog-safe shampoo and conditioner. Bathtime is a great opportunity to teach your puppy to be calm and respectful. They do not have to *love* bathtime; they simply need to *tolerate* it. Your dog will most likely love swimming and tolerate bathing and that is okay.

BRUSHING

Your puppy will probably not shed very much for the first several months. This is because they have their puppy coat, which does not shed as much as their adult coat. This does not mean you should not brush them! Brushing your young puppy teaches them to be tolerant and respectful while being brushed. Get them used to the brush now so that they are well-behaved later on when they are older and bigger. Biting the brush is not allowed. They must lay on their side and stay there or stand still until you release them. It is okay to give your puppy a food reward or gentle pets for good behavior.

Brushing your dog is a good opportunity to feel all over your dog's body to check for lumps, bumps, and scrapes. Staying on top of your dog's brushing also helps to keep your dog comfortable and unmatted. Use a brush that is appropriate for your dog's coat. If you have a double-coated dog, *never shave them*—it ruins the coat—and never use a brush that rips out the top coat.

NAIL TRIMS

You want to teach your puppy to tolerate both a nail clipper and a Dremel, so that they are able to handle both methods of nail trims when they are older. I prefer to use nail clippers first to get the length off, and then I use a Dremel to get nails shorter and round-out the edges.

When clipping your dog's nails, the goal is to get the nails short without hitting the quick. To do this, put the clippers at a forty-five degree angle and take your time. Go slow. Look online for a visual of how best to trim your dog's nails and avoid hitting the quick. If the quick is accidentally cut, the nail will start to bleed. Use styptic powder to stop the bleeding.

I clip *weekly* to keep nails short. The rule of thumb is, "*If you hear them, clip them*!" This means that if you can hear your puppy's nails on hardwood or vinyl flooring, it is time for a trim! Long nails are one of my pet peeves because they are painful for dogs to live with. Do your dog a favor and keep their nails SHORT.

TEETH

Dental hygiene affects overall health. If you feed raw, the raw bones will help keep plaque off their teeth. If you feed kibble, you will need to brush your dog's teeth on a regular basis to keep them clean and plaque-free. You can start by using your finger to get your dog used to the brushing sensation, then switch to a toothbrush with doggie toothpaste.

CLEANING EARS

I do not clean my dogs' ears often, but I do clean them. I like to get build-up out of their ears, but I do not go deep into their ear canal. Use a cotton ball and gently wipe out your puppy's ears. Use one cotton ball per ear—never mixing them up—to ensure that you are not transferring what is in one ear to the other ear. If your dog is shaking their head often, they may have an ear infection and will need to visit the veterinarian.

Do not allow water to get in your dog's ears during a bath.

OTHER HEALTH CONSIDERATIONS

Below are other health considerations for your dog. These are concepts for you to consider, not medical advice. I want to mention them to you so that you can make informed decisions for your dog's health and wellness, as opposed to going with the status quo.

SPAYING AND NEUTERING

I have worked with a lot of rescues and respect why most of them recommend pediatric spay and neuter. For dog owners who can be responsible, I advocate for keeping dogs intact for life, or until they are fully grown, for health reasons.

When a female dog is spayed or a male dog is neutered, their growth hormones are removed. This is unnatural and can lead to health issues such as urinary incontinence and early-onset arthritis.

I spayed Zoey when she was a puppy and soon after regretted it. Now that I know better, I do better and leave my dogs intact for life. Intact is best!

If you are going to spay or neuter, it is best to wait until your dog is twelve to twenty-four months of age, depending on their size and breed. Do your research to determine the best age for this life-changing operation.

VACCINATIONS

I believe in minimal vaccines and in using a delayed vaccination schedule. This means I only give mandatory vaccines and spread them out as much as possible. I do not give optional vaccines that are not required by law.

After a year of age, I do titer testing in place of additional vaccines. This tests for antibodies in your dog's blood and is a great way to know whether or not your dog needs booster shots, such as rabies. The more informed you are when making decisions about your dog's health, the better!

Many dogs do not need nearly as many vaccines as they are being given and some dogs die from over-vaccination! One of my good clients lost her two-year-old golden retriever, who was a therapy dog, to the rabies vaccine. He began having uncontrollable seizures and they had to put him down.

A little research goes a long way. Your dog is counting on you to do what is best!

BLOAT

As discussed in Chapter 10, if you have a dog, especially a deep-chested dog like a German shepherd, you need to be aware of gastric dilatation-volvulus (GDV), also called "bloat." It is a life-threatening condition that can be fatal in a matter of hours. Bloat is when your dog's stomach twists and gasses build up. It kills major organs and can be deadly even if operated on.

The best way to prevent bloat is to feed one meal per day, in the evening, one hour or more after activity. After eating, do not allow your dog to be active. Resting after meals is best.

Eating or drinking large amounts, before or after exercise, can also lead to bloat. Only allow your dog to have a few sips of water before and after vigorous exercise. After exercise, once they stop panting, they can have more water.

I am passionate about educating dog owners about bloat because one of my own dogs, a German shepherd named Duke, bloated many years ago at just two years of age. If not for my knowledge, quick thinking, and on-hand first aid kit, he might have died. I am very grateful for the canine first aid and CPR training I have received throughout my career.

Valor K9 Academy Online offers a canine first aid course that could help you save your dog's life someday. Be sure to check it out!

HEALTH TESTING

Research indicates that approximately 75 percent of dogs are at risk or carriers for genetic health conditions. For this reason, I recommend doing a full DNA panel on your dog so that you have as much information about your dog as possible. DNA testing is relatively inexpensive and deep-dives into your dog's ancestry, breed/s, and genetic health. This information can change the way you and your veterinarian care for your dog on a regular basis and during an emergency situation.

Embark, Wisdom Panel, and UC Davis offer health testing for dogs.

If you can afford it, I also recommend X-raying your dog's hips, elbows, and spine at a year of age. This will help you know if your dog has healthy or unhealthy joints, which could impact their exercise and training regimen. Do your research and choose a veterinarian that is skilled at positioning for X-rays. Positioning makes all the difference when it comes to getting a good look at orthopedics.

The more you know, the more proactive you can be!

ANNUAL BLOOD WORK

Another thing I recommend doing is annual blood work. This gives insight into your dog's overall health and wellness and can help catch problems early on before they develop into major or life-threatening issues.

Your veterinarian can tell you which blood panel is best for your dog based on your dog's age and health status.

PET HEALTH INSURANCE

Accidents happen! If you do not have the funds saved to pay for emergency surgery, you may look into dog pet insurance. It covers anything from routine physicals to injuries, illnesses, and vaccinations, depending on the plan you select.

There are multiple companies offering pet health insurance with plans designed to fit your budget and lifestyle.

CANINE FIRST AID KIT

I highly recommend keeping a canine first aid kit on hand, stocked with all the essentials. Know what is in it and how to use it. Having the right items and knowledge could save your dog's life someday!

My first aid skills have come in handy for dogs who would have overheated, had minor injuries, or needed immediate medical care. At the very least, keep a pet thermometer on hand so that you can quickly take your dog's temperature if they are acting ill. Knowing if a dog is running a fever is valuable information to have. Always know where the closest emergency veterinarian is. Save their contact information and address in your phone so that you have them ready in the event of an emergency.

VK9 FIRST AID AND CPR COURSE

I cannot stress enough the importance of canine first aid and CPR training. In our course, you will learn preventative care for baseline treatment, how to conduct a physical exam, canine casualty care for emergency situations, the best techniques to apply potentially life-saving first aid and CPR, and how to build and use your canine first aid kit.

Our course is taught by a Special Forces K9 medic. The training could save your dog's life someday.

Chapter Summary

Your dog is counting on you to take good care of them. A healthy dog is a happy dog. Use the information in this chapter to make informed decisions for your dog. They will thank you for it in the long run.

14.

PROBLEMS AND SOLUTIONS

"We cannot solve our problems with the same thinking we used when we created them."
—Albert Einstein

Puppies are living, breathing creatures. They are not robots and, despite your best efforts, things might not always go according to plan. While raising your puppy, if you hit a few bumps in the road, you might need help working through them. If you do, this chapter is for you.

This entire chapter is dedicated to identifying, understanding, and solving dozens of common puppy problems. I have seen it all, and I am here to help!

Read the first part of this chapter, then jump to the issue you are having. If you never need the rest of the chapter, great. If you want to read it to learn more about how dogs think and how to prevent problems, that is a great idea too.

Barring genetics, every problem has a solution. Remember that!

UNDERSTANDING PROBLEMS

When a client comes to me with a puppy problem, the first thing I do is identify it. What is it that the puppy is doing? If you can name it, you can fix it.

Next, I ask questions and dig deeper to understand the root causes of the problem. The root cause is the *why*. Why is the puppy doing what they are doing? What is happening in that puppy's home, environment, or routine that is preceding, causing, or enabling the unwanted behavior?

Lastly, based on those root causes, I come up with solutions.

Most problems stem from the following root causes:

- insufficient physical exercise
- insufficient mental stimulation
- insufficient training
- too much freedom
- too much crate time
- not working for food
- inconsistency from one family member to the next
- poor communication

By fixing those issues, you are almost guaranteed to fix the problem.

Overall, when a problem rears its ugly head, the simple truth is the owner messed up somewhere along the line. Most puppy problems are *owner problems.* Not always, but usually. Puppies, like kids, are a product of their environment.

Genetics plays a role too, and in some cases the problem is genetic. Genetic problems require a lot of work and management to prevent them from happening again. Managing behavior is hard for most dog owners.

The good news is, in most cases, genetics is not the issue. In most cases, the puppy is just naughty and needs to learn what they can and cannot do. Simple!

Let's discuss the science behind problem-solving.

COUNTERCONDITIONING

Let's say your puppy has had some bad experiences. Maybe a bike fell on them, kids pulled their tail, a gunshot startled them, yada yada yada. Time for damage control. Time to do some counterconditioning.

Counterconditioning is the process by which we reverse negative conditioning that has been done to a puppy. In layman's terms, it is our attempt to blot out bad experiences to give our puppy a fresh start.

Counterconditioning is designed to replace negative responses to stimuli with positive ones. It is simple, but it is not easy. What makes it hard is that it is a slow and methodical process that requires pre-planning and considerable effort from all parties involved. There is no instant gratification in counterconditioning. You just have to stay the course and hope for the best.

Give yourself grace. Counterconditioning can be difficult. As long as you are seeing progress, keep doing what you are doing.

DESENSITIZATION

Counterconditioning is usually done in correlation with desensitization. *Desensitization* is the process by which dogs are exposed to a trigger at a very low intensity level, repeatedly and over time, in a manner that is not overwhelming and does not create a fear response.

Desensitization essentially means breaking it down into bite-sized pieces. The goal is to figure out how to make the trigger less threatening. A trigger that is physically small or not moving is usually a great place to start.

Keep in mind, in both of these processes, you are literally rewiring your dog's brain. You are changing their thinking. Embrace it and do your best!

A WORD ON EXTINCTION

Any time you are trying to stop a behavior that is a habit and has been reinforced in the past, you are likely going to run into something called "extinction." Extinction has two forms: intentional extinction and unintentional extinction.

If your dog has a problem behavior that you want to stop, you are going to put intentional extinction into effect. *Intentional extinction* is when you stop reinforcing (rewarding) an unwanted behavior in hopes that it will eventually go away.

Your puppy will probably throw a fit. Their behavior during this time of extinction might get worse before it gets better. We call this an "extinction burst." An extinction burst is like a volcano. Your dog's behavior erupts into a behavior that is far worse than before because they are fighting the extinction. They *like* the behavior they were doing before, because it produced a reward, so they do not *want* to stop doing it and they are not going down without a fight!

For example, if your dog begs from the table because you give in, but you suddenly stop doing so, they are going to throw a fit. "*I want table scraps, and I want them now*!" Instead of softly whining for food like they did before, they might bark, howl, and throw a tantrum. Bad dog!

That, my friend, is an extinction burst. The good news is that usually after a burst, the dog's behavior does, indeed, improve. They realize that the tantrum did not work and give up.

Providing an alternative behavior, like putting your dog on the place bed or in the crate during dinner instead of letting them sit next to your chair, helps tremendously with stopping unwanted behaviors and *prevents* the extinction burst from happening. It is the most effective way to extinguish behavior without all the drama.

Regardless of how your dog does, stay the course. Do not give up. You *will* win. Trust the process.

Unintentional extinction is where you stop reinforcing a *wanted* behavior, like obedience to a command, so your dog stops doing it. We talk about this more in the next chapter.

THE PROBLEMS

Here are twenty-five common puppy problems. With each of the problems below—written in alphabetical order—I name the problem, point out common root causes, and offer up solutions that are 95 percent likely to fix the issues. I say 95 percent because no two dogs are the same and sometimes life throws us curveballs.

If you think your dog is in the 5 percent range, then a virtual one-on-one coaching session is a good idea. We can troubleshoot and solve the problems you are having together.

1. BEGGING (FOR FOOD)

If your puppy is begging for food, chances are it is because they have been fed (by someone) from the table or fed food outside of a training session. Dogs do not beg for food that they don't think they are ever going to get. Once they get some, that is all they can think about, especially if they are highly food-motivated.

You need to start by talking to everyone in the household to see if anyone has been feeding your puppy table scraps. Whoever is doing it needs to stop. From there, start by putting your puppy in the crate during meals to break the cycle of expecting table scraps during mealtimes.

After a week or so, try putting your puppy on the place bed at least ten feet away from the kitchen table but still in sight. Practice tethered decompression during the meal and supervise your puppy to ensure they are not barking, whining, digging, or chewing the slip lead. If they are, it is a sign that they need more physical exercise, mental stimulation, and training prior to being put on the place bed.

If people in public want to give your puppy a treat, it is best to politely tell them "No." You do not want your puppy to be rude or pushy in public.

If you have any other dogs in the house who beg, their begging needs to be addressed as well. You cannot feed one dog from the table and not the other and expect the dog who is left out to be okay with it. Dogs model behavior. Fairness is key.

2. CHASING SMALL ANIMALS

If your puppy is chasing small animals—like cats, chickens, and squirrels—they probably have a decent amount of prey drive. Prey drive is a dog's subconscious urge to capture and kill prey, remember? This is discussed in Chapter 1.

Prey drive is not a problem. It is unchecked and uncontrolled prey drive that can quickly spiral out of control. Prey drive, like any drive, needs to be controlled. There is a time and a place for everything!

Let's say your puppy's problem is chasing cats. Chasing cats is fun! Step one: put the slip lead on your puppy. Your puppy cannot chase the cat when they are leashed to you because you can stop them right away. Do not let your puppy chase the cat or else the reward for chasing will outweigh any correction you give.

Next, you need to increase your puppy's motivation. If your puppy is not working for food, they need to be.

Go back to the basics and make sure your foundation obedience is good. Your puppy should be luring, engaging (making eye contact), and following basic commands with ease.

Provide your puppy with sufficient physical exercise, then bring them in the vicinity of the cat (distance is your friend) and work with them. Keep their mind engaged and their body moving. Do not allow them to fixate on the cat or chase it (obviously). If they move towards it, give them a swift "pop" with the slip lead. They need to understand very clearly that chasing cats is not allowed. If your puppy struggles with this, tire them out more and/or add more distance from the cat. A slow-moving or primarily stationary cat is best for starters. Perhaps someone else in the household can hold the cat while you work with the dog.

Movement is key. Keep your puppy's mind engaged and their body moving. Start small and work towards bigger goals, like moving closer to the cat and doing stationary obedience in the presence of the cat.

The number-one rule for dogs with prey drive is that they should not be allowed to chase in the first place. Be consistent with this and you will thrive! In the Good Dog program, we add a training collar for on- and off-leash obedience. The training collar is *magic* for dogs with high prey drive. It puts a stop to their unwanted behavior once and for all.

3. CHASING VEHICLES OR SHADOWS

If your puppy is chasing vehicles or shadows, they are bored and have been left to their own devices too frequently and for too long. It is time to put the slip lead back on and work hard on meeting your dog's three basic needs (physical exercise, mental stimulation, and training). Once you have done that, the second your dog starts to chase something, put a stop to it by telling them a firm "No," then popping them hard with the slip lead. If your pup continues to give chase, pop several times while backing away from whatever it is that they are barking at. Whenever possible, put more distance between the stimulus and your dog to set them up for success.

Distance is your friend.

4. COPROPHAGIA (EATING POOP)

If your puppy is eating their own poop or another animal's poop, it is called "coprophagia." It is actually a pretty common problem with puppies, especially in multi-dog households.

There can be many explanations for this behavior. Curiosity, boredom, hunger, or lack of nutrients and an unclean living situation are the top causes. Puppies who are bored and left in the yard to play might decide to investigate, play with, or eat poop. This can lead to a habit of eating poop. Other puppies might eat poop because they are hungry or their bodies are lacking nutrients. Puppies who came from unclean environments, like backyard breeders or puppy mills, might be in the habit of eating their poop because it is left in the crate with them.

First and foremost, you need to pick up all poop in your yard. Next, you need to double-check and make sure that your puppy is a healthy weight and that the food they are eating is nutritious and providing them with the proper balance of nutrients that they need for growth.

From there, every time you take your puppy outside, you need to take them on a leash. Every time! Watch them as they poop and be ready to pull them away from the poop as soon as they finish. Do not allow them to poop then turn around and sniff it. Chances are, they are going to try to eat it! Preventing them from eating poop is key because it breaks the cycle of coprophagia. The same goes for playtime in the yard. All poop must be picked up first, and your puppy needs to be kept on a leash so that you can immediately intervene and pull them away from poop after they go potty.

If your puppy is pooping in the crate and eating it, you need to clean their crate and make sure it's odor-free. Afterwards, focus on providing your puppy with more frequent potty breaks outside. Control their portion sizes during training sessions so that they can hold it longer in the crate in the event you're unable to potty them when they might need to go. If they do poop in their crate, take them outside immediately and clean their crate before putting them back in it.

If you ever see your puppy trying to eat poop, yell "No!" and do whatever it takes to keep your puppy from eating it. Your reaction should startle your puppy so they stop in their tracks, which is exactly what you want.

The key to overcoming coprophagia is preventing your puppy from ever wanting or needing to eat poop again. By meeting their needs for physical exercise, mental stimulation, and training, and by ensuring they are getting quality food and frequent, supervised potty breaks, you should be able to break the habit in a matter of weeks. This is something that can become a lifelong problem if it is not addressed swiftly and correctly.

5. COUNTER SURFING

"Counter surfing" is a lighthearted way of saying "puppies who jump on the counter and steal food." Usually, puppies who do this have too much freedom, are off leash when they should not be, or have been set up to fail by owners who leave something delicious (like steak or bacon) on the counter. Dogs obey their noses and go where it tells them to go. Counter surfing is a crime of opportunity.

Oftentimes, dogs who are fed table scraps or scraps from the kitchen during meal prep have a greater tendency to become counter surfers. This is why not feeding your dog scraps from the kitchen counter or dining room table is important. Do not put the thought into their head in the first place! Food should be saved for later and put directly into your dog's bowl during meals. I feed meals in the garage, well away from the kitchen.

To stop counter surfing, you need to focus on three things: relinquishing freedom, putting the slip lead on at all times in the house, and not leaving food on the counter. From there, you can set up supervised training sessions where you intentionally put something on the counter, walk your puppy up to it, and if your puppy even so much as *thinks* about jumping up to get it, yell "No!" and pop them hard with the slip lead. It should startle them enough to make them leave in a hurry.

As your puppy matures, you can begin to incrementally give freedom back and see what your dog does with it. Do they make good choices or do they commit the crime again?

In some cases, staying on a slip lead is required until the next level of training is accomplished. Using an e-collar is a game-changer for dogs who counter surf. With it, you are able to give a high-level, God-given correction when your dog thinks no one is looking and tries to steal food off the counter. They will never do it again, guaranteed.

Wait until your dog is six months of age before introducing the e-collar. We cover e-collar training in the Valor K9 Academy Online Good Dog course!

6. CRATE ANXIETY

If your puppy is barking, whining, crying, digging, or trying to chew their way out of the crate, they have crate anxiety. Keep in mind, early on with young puppies, barking and crying in the crate is normal. But if the behavior continues, persists, or worsens, you have a problem on your hands.

Start by reviewing Chapter 6 on crate training. Are you following all the tips and tricks in that chapter? Meeting your puppy's needs for The Big Three and providing a crate that is safe and den-like are the most important steps to crate training. All too often, the number-one cause of crate anxiety is owners not doing enough while their puppies are out of the crate and then putting their puppies in the crate when they are energetic and need to have their needs met.

It is really important the first few weeks to try your best to (safely) tire your puppy out before putting them in the crate. When all else fails, follow my instructions for correcting your puppy for unwanted behavior like barking and whining. Going in and smacking the top of the crate or hitting the crate door with your hand usually does the trick. Your timing is key. Make sure you are correcting your puppy at the first sign of anxiety. Do not wait until later when they have gotten carried away.

Do not—I repeat, DO NOT—go in and take your puppy out of the crate when they are whining and crying. This teaches them that crying gets them out of the crate. You need to let them cry it out and stick to your guns. You can undo weeks of successful crate training by teaching your puppy that barking gets them out of the crate.

Other solutions for crate anxiety include getting a new crate (that is a different shape or size so that your puppy has no prior associations with that crate) or keeping your puppy awake the entire time they are out of the crate (and for hours on end) so that they are completely exhausted by the time you put them in the crate. Typically, you only need two or three good crate sessions to overcome crate anxiety. If your problem worsens or does not get better, seek help.

Do not give up on crate training. Learning to be calm, quiet, and comfortable in the crate is a skill that all puppies need to have. It helps with every aspect of puppy training. The juice is worth the squeeze!

7. DEMAND-BARKING

Demand-barking is when your puppy is bored, excited, or otherwise unsettled, so they *look at you* and *bark at you*. They want *something*—food, attention, playtime—and they are not going to stop barking until they get what they want. (Or so they think.) Demand-barking is a common problem with older puppies whose owners have not trained them yet so they are training their owners instead!

Dogs demand-bark because it works. They get what they want… usually. So, naturally the solution is to not give your dog what they want or, better yet, give them exactly the opposite of what they want, a correction! First, start by setting your puppy up for success. What is the situation in which they demand-bark? Before putting your puppy in that situation, exercise them and do a few training sessions with them. By meeting their needs, you have a greater likelihood of nipping the problem in the bud.

From there, put them in the situation in which they bark. Have the slip lead on them, and when they bark at you—the *second* they start to bark—do not say anything, do not look at them, just pop them *hard* with the slip lead. If they bark again, pop them again, this time even harder than the last. You want your puppy to know that barking does not work *and gets them nowhere*.

Oftentimes, in situations where a puppy has learned to demand-bark, they will try several times before they give up and settle down. This is why our program is structured to cover lots of foundation training first, before working on tethered decompression, which is commonly when demand-barking occurs. By then, you have a good working relationship with your puppy and something like this is much easier to correct and put a stop to, as opposed to starting fresh with an untrained puppy who knows nothing and does not respect you yet.

Other times, puppies demand-bark from their crate. This is because they want something or because they are anticipating something (like food or playtime) and they are trying to force your hand. You need to ensure your puppy's routine is more unpredictable, they are working for their food and not receiving a free meal in a dish, and, if your puppy does demand-bark from the crate, the only attention they get from you is a firm "No!" and a smack on the top of the crate. Do not talk to your puppy, take them out of the crate, or give them what they want.

Demand-barking is pretty easy to fix in a single training session. Stick to your guns!

8. DESTRUCTIVE CHEWING

Is your puppy chewing something they are not supposed to, such as the rug, their leash, or your shoe?

Destructive chewing is a sign of boredom. It happens when a puppy's basic needs for physical exercise, mental stimulation, and training have not been met. It also sometimes occurs from fourteen to eighteen weeks of age when puppies are teething—losing their baby teeth and getting adult teeth in their place. Their mouths hurt, and they need something to chew on to pacify the pain. If your puppy is teething, be sure to provide plenty of bones to chew on. Always leave a bone in their crate and have a bone available during tethered decompression so that they can have something to do when the urge hits.

In all other cases, puppies who are destructively chewing simply need to be kept on a leash and have their needs met. You can pop your puppy with the slip lead when they start to chew something they should not, and they should get your message loud and clear.

Like counter surfing, destructive chewing is usually a crime of opportunity. Make sure your home is sufficiently puppy-proofed and that nothing is left in or on top of the crate that your puppy is not allowed to chew on. Supervision and proper management are essential.

Break the habit—prevent chewing—and you should be golden in no time.

9. DIARRHEA

If your puppy has diarrhea, rule out medical reasons first. If your puppy has bloody diarrhea, black, tarry stools, a fever, pale gums, or discomfort or pain, is vomiting, has diarrhea lasting more than a day, or if you think they may have swallowed a foreign body or toxic substance, contact your veterinarian's office and notify them of the situation. More than likely, they will ask you to bring your puppy in for a quick exam. If you are able to bring a small stool sample in, along with your puppy, that is always helpful.

Diarrhea can be caused by a number of things: diet change or food intolerance, bacterial infection, viral infection, ingestion of garbage, toxins or foreign bodies, parasites, and/or stress.

Once you rule out medical causes, here is a six-step treatment plan:

1. Fast your dog for twelve to twenty-four hours before feeding the next meal. Give water throughout the day.
2. When the fast is over, feed them cooked squash or pumpkin and meat broth for twenty-four to forty-eight hours. Use enough broth to achieve a runny, porridge consistency.
3. Transition to a lean meat and veggie blend for one to two days before switching back to regular food.
4. Keep your dog well hydrated.
5. Give your dog a canine-specific prebiotic, probiotic, and digestive support supplement made with non-dairy, organic, and natural ingredients to replenish the intestinal flora.
6. Gradually transition to a regular diet within two to three days.

If your pup's diarrhea continues or worsens, contact your veterinarian.

10. DIGGING

If your puppy is digging holes in your backyard, it is likely due to a number of reasons. First, they are bored. They have been left in the yard with nothing to do, so they have come up with a new hobby. Bored dogs are usually bad dogs!

Second, their hearing is better than yours and chances are they hear moles in the ground. They are chewing up your sprinkler system because they are trying to locate those pesky moles!

Third, they are digging because it provides them with a great feeling of satisfaction. Digging is a good workout, and dogs who dig tend to keep digging unless you stop them.

For me, I allow my dogs to dig in the open field far from the house. They can dig and hunt for mice to their heart's content. I don't mind it one bit, but they are *not* allowed to dig anywhere near the house or in the landscaping.

To stop your puppy from digging, you need to first increase their physical exercise, mental stimulation, and training. They are digging because they are bored and they are bored because you are not doing a good job meeting their needs. Start there.

Next, head out to the yard (without your puppy). Fill in all the holes with dog poop, then cover them with dirt. This is going to create a negative association with the holes for your puppy (provided coprophagia—#4 on this list—is not currently a problem for them).

For the next several weeks, every time your puppy goes outside, take them on the leash and supervise them. If they *think* about digging or start to dig, stop them immediately. Yell. Pop the leash. Pull them away from the hole. They need to understand that digging is *not* okay.

Most dogs, once corrected for digging, do not dig again. At least not for a while. When your puppy is six months or older, you can use the e-collar to give a high-level, God-given correction for digging. They will stop dead in their tracks and never dig again.

Please do not try this at home until you learn how to properly use an e-collar.

11. DOG AGGRESSION

If your puppy seems dangerous around other dogs or has hurt a dog in the past—puncturing the dog and/or drawing blood—then they might have dog aggression. I say "*might*" because it is very rare to see true dog aggression in puppies.

Resource guarding (problem #24) and fear reactivity (problem #23) are common in puppies but not dog aggression. Usually with true dog aggression, there is a strong genetic component to the behavior that can be hard to pinpoint.

Most puppies in these situations are reactive, not aggressive. If you think your puppy might have dog aggression problems, the best thing you can do is work in person and hands-on with an experienced, professional dog trainer who has successfully worked with aggressive dogs in the past. Make sure the trainer has access to a pack of stable, balanced dogs who can help your puppy work through their problems. My dogs have helped me rehabilitate hundreds of fearful, reactive, and aggressive dogs over the course of my career. Their help is invaluable.

At the end of the day, you may not be 100 percent successful. A good trainer can modify behavior, but no one can change genetics. More than likely, you will need a good management plan in place to keep your dog out of trouble around other dogs.

12. EXCESSIVE BARKING

What is considered excessive barking? It depends on who you ask. For me, excessive barking is anything more than a few barks. It involves a dog repeatedly barking for prolonged periods of time. This can occur in the car, the crate, the backyard, and everywhere in between.

Excessive barking is also referred to as "boredom barking." A dog who barks a lot is a dog who is bored. They have nothing to do and have become easily stimulated by their environment. They have given themselves a job to do and that job is barking.

If this is a problem you are having with your puppy, the solution is simple. Your puppy needs more physical exercise, mental stimulation, training, and structure. You need to focus on meeting your dog's needs so that they do not feel the need to bark nonstop. If it is helpful, refer back to Chapter 3 to find out which piece of the puzzle you might be missing in your dog's everyday care and training routine.

It is normal for puppies to begin alert barking—barking when people come to the door, cars pull up the driveway, or they hear a strange sound—when they reach five to seven months of age. Anything before that is likely boredom barking and needs to be nixed straight away.

13. EXCESSIVE LICKING

If your dog is licking their paws or feet, they might have an environmental allergy or food intolerance. Contact your veterinarian and get your dog in for an exam.

If your dog is constantly licking you, your hands, your feet, or someone else, their licking is a sign of an obsessive-compulsive behavior. Usually this behavior is allowed and/or reinforced by the owner (or person being licked) and continued frequently over a long period of time.

To stop excessive licking, start by putting a slip lead on your dog. Pop them every time they start to lick. Focus your energy on keeping them engaged and working with them often throughout the day. Train them. Exercise them. Challenge their brain. If they are bored, licking is their way of coming up with a "job" to do. It is no different from dogs who chase shadows or bark at moving vehicles. They are bored and need a job.

It is your job to give your dog a job to do. Just make sure it is one you like! Dogs with obsessive-compulsive behaviors usually benefit greatly from working in a job their breed was created for. Border collies, for example, love to herd and are very mentally and physically satisfied when they are allowed to herd sheep and do what they were bred to do. Bloodhounds love to track. Pointers love to hunt. German shepherds are versatile working dogs who love a good challenge.

Licking and other OCD behaviors need to be addressed right away before they get worse.

Be very mindful to not reinforce licking in any way, shape, or form. Correct your dog and do not put them back in that same situation where they might fail again in the future.

14. EXCESSIVE WHINING

Excessive whining is typically much like problem #7 (demand-barking). Your puppy wants something and they are not going to stop until they get what they want. In other instances, excessive whining can be due to separation anxiety.

Puppies who whine endlessly on the place bed or in the crate, for example, are usually puppies who suffer from separation anxiety or are having a hard time with crate training. They are uncomfortable being away from their people and want you to come closer to them. They are hoping that, by whining, you will give them attention. Be careful because if you do, you are reinforcing their behavior and it will continue.

If your puppy is whining in the crate, see problem #6 (crate anxiety) for solutions.

If you want to put a stop to a puppy who is whining for attention, you need to first meet your puppy's needs for physical exercise, mental stimulation, and training. Work your puppy hard and try your best to safely tire them out. With the slip lead on, put them in the situation where they are most likely to whine and when they whine, pop them hard with the slip lead. Do not look at them, talk to them, or give them any form of attention. Just a hard pop on the leash. You want them to realize that whining gets them one thing—a correction—and that is not what they want. When they learn that they do not get rewarded for the behavior, they will stop. If they do not and they are away from you, you might be dealing with problem #25 (separation anxiety).

15. JUMPING ON PEOPLE

If your puppy is jumping on people, go back to Chapter 7. Where did you go wrong? Jumping is almost always the result of too much freedom combined with too much stimulation. Puppies jump when they are excited and when people let them jump. They definitely jump up when people reach down and pet them. Are you (or someone else) reinforcing your dog's unwanted jumping problem? Identify who the culprit is, then ask them to please stop because their behavior is negating your training.

I have my "Five-Year-Old/Grandmother Rule." Very simply, if you do not want your dog jumping on a five-year-old child or an elderly grandmother, do not let them jump on you. I never let my dogs jump on me. It is not cute and is unacceptable in every way, shape, and form.

Exercise your puppy, put a slip lead on them, and practice manners with people. Something has gone awry, and it is time to give your puppy more practice. Teach them what you *want* them to do on top of teaching them what you *do not* want them to do. They need to see both sides of the coin to fully understand what is acceptable and what is not.

16. HUMPING

Humping is usually a sign of dominance, testosterone, or pheromones that are in full gear. As your puppy matures, especially if you have a male dog, you might start to see some humping behaviors. This is normal, but that does not mean it is acceptable or should be allowed.

If your dog is humping someone or something, put the leash on them and give them a hard pop. Correct them for it! They need to know that you do not like and will not allow such behavior.

Set your pup up for success by supervising them at all times, especially in situations where they are prone to hump, and be ready to give a well-timed correction.

During a play session, most other dogs will usually move, sit down, or snap at a dog that starts to hump them. This is fine, but it is still your job to step in and stop your dog and vice versa. Other dogs should not have to do that for you. If your dog humps the wrong dog, that dog might attack them for it. Most dogs are tolerant of a young, hormonal puppy humping them, but not all dogs are. Do not assume your puppy is going to get away unscathed.

17. HYPERACTIVITY

If your dog is hyperactive—excessively energetic and unable to sit still—you might rule out medical reasons first. Is your dog eating a nutritious diet or is their food full of cheap fillers and simple carbohydrates? Diet influences behavior. Check out Chapter 13 if you are unsure of the quality of food your dog is on. Many dog owners see a *significant* change in their dog's overall behavior when they switch to a high-quality food.

From there, if that is not the solution, take a look at your dog's lifestyle. Are you meeting their needs for physical exercise, mental stimulation, and training? Is your dog getting enough breed-specific exercise? Do they have free access to toys? (If they do, they should not!) Do they have too much freedom? Are they playing in the house instead of only playing outside? Remember, calm in the house; play is for outside. Most importantly, what are *you* doing when your dog acts up? Are you reinforcing it in any way or are you grabbing the leash, popping them, and putting them next to you in the Art of Doing Nothing? Most dogs who are naughty on leash or in the house are doing it *because they can*, plain and simple. If you do not like it, then stop it. Anything you allow, you are effectively reinforcing.

If all of that does not fix the "hyperactivity," ask yourself, "Is my dog hyperactive or are they just fine but I'm in over my head?" It is all too common for people to buy a puppy out of impulse and then learn very quickly that the dog is too much for them, especially when they turn out to be a working dog or a high-drive dog. In such cases, if you are unwilling or unable to give your dog the exercise and training that *they want, need, and deserve*, then it is time to do the selfless thing and find them an owner that will.

Most high-energy dogs are not bad dogs. They are just in homes that are not well-suited for them. The right dog in the right home thrives. Ask yourself, "Why isn't my dog thriving? *Is it me or the dog?*"

18. FEAR OF DOGS

When meeting another dog, if your dog is cowering, shaking, tucking their tail under their belly, snapping at the other dog, or trying to hide behind you, they are afraid. Fear is usually due to lack of socialization, poor socialization, or a significant bad experience with another dog (such as an attack).

Keep in mind, if your puppy is somewhere around eight weeks of age, or six to eight months of age, they might be going through a fear period. In this case, they are not actually afraid of dogs; their brain is just rewiring and it is best to avoid dogs for a while.

If your puppy is not in a fear period and they are truly afraid of other dogs, you have your work cut out for you. Your first task is to find someone who has a calm, social, balanced dog who is willing to ignore your puppy. Try going for a walk together (you, your puppy, the dog's owner, and the dog) and allow your puppy to familiarize themselves with the other dog from a distance. This approach allows your puppy to settle in and takes the pressure off your puppy to go say hi to a dog they probably do not want to say hi to.

If the other dog is truly calm and balanced, they will ignore your puppy and give your puppy time to settle in before saying hi, if they do at all. My personal dogs ignore timid puppies and do not approach until they feel the puppy is ready for it. Give your puppy praise, affection, and treats for calm, confident behavior *only*. If they are nervous, do not coddle them, reward them, or reinforce their fearful state of mind in any way. Movement is key. Keep moving, do not stop, and do not allow the other dog to approach or intimidate your puppy in any way. The goal of this session is for your puppy to get comfortable enough to casually sniff the other dog and let that dog sniff them. That is when you end the session and celebrate your small win!

For sessions like this, it is always a good idea to tire your puppy out ahead of time—before the walk—so that they have less physical energy and can reach a calm state of mind more quickly.

Your goal is to provide your puppy with multiple sessions where they are in the presence of calm, balanced dogs. This will help them get over their fear and create new pathways in their brain. Over time, your puppy will be able to handle more excitable and energetic dogs who are not as calm. The goal is for them to be willing to say hi to other balanced dogs and warm up more quickly to new dogs.

Often, it is hard to find calm, balanced dogs. A good trainer will own them and will have access to more good dogs—and clients—who may be willing to meet up with you. Do some digging and do not give up. Your puppy is only young once. Address their fears now to give them the best quality of life later.

19. FEAR OF PEOPLE

Does your puppy cower, growl, bark, snap at, or try to run away from people? So long as they are not in a fear period and this is a persistent problem, then it sounds like you have a puppy who is afraid of people.

Fear of people usually stems from a lack of positive and neutral socialization with people and an overall lack of confidence. It is rarely due to a bad experience or abuse like most people incorrectly assume.

Start by addressing the confidence problem. Go to Chapter 9 (Socialization and Exposure) and work on exposing your puppy to more new surfaces. I have found that surfaces are great for confidence building. A puppy who is fearful of new surfaces usually has other fear problems. Build their confidence with surfaces and that confidence will spill over to other areas where they might need confidence building.

Spend a week, at minimum, on new surfaces, while having your puppy work for food. Like the approach to problem #18 (fear of dogs), you need to find a few calm people to help you with your puppy's confidence building. Involving one person per session, ask someone to stand about fifteen to twenty feet from you. Work with your puppy and see if your puppy is comfortable or uncomfortable in the presence of that other person. If your puppy is comfortable, move a little closer. Find your puppy's threshold (the distance from the person at which your puppy changes their behavior or shows fear).

Perhaps you already know your puppy's threshold. Once you identify the threshold, continue working with your puppy. Do basic skills like luring, Name Game, two-treat recall, and Preheeling. Work on manners around people. Do not ask your puppy to approach the person to "go say hi." Neutrality is the goal. You want your puppy to learn to be comfortable in the presence of a stranger. After many sessions, you will be able to work towards creating more positive associations with people.

Give the stranger high-value treats that your puppy loves (not kibble) and ask the stranger to toss them in the direction of your puppy while ignoring your puppy completely ("No touch, no talk, no eye contact"). This neutrality oftentimes helps puppies step out of their comfort zone and eventually approach the stranger to take treats out of their hand. That is what you want!

Over time your puppy will be able to take the treat from the stranger's hand and, before long, the stranger (who is now your puppy's friend) can take your puppy's leash, do some basic obedience exercises like Name Game, or even work on new surfaces with them, just like you've been doing. The idea here is that you want your puppy to realize that strangers are not going to put pressure on them. They do not need to be afraid because strangers equal good things (food, training, activities).

If your puppy has a bite history or is otherwise unstable or a dangerous, contact a trainer who can work with you in person to address your puppy's aggression. It is wrong to ask people to put themselves in harm's way to help with an aggressive dog. That kind of training is best left to skilled, experienced professionals.

20. FEAR OF SIGHTS, SOUNDS, AND/OR SURFACES

If your dog is not in a fear period and is showing an obvious fear of new sights, sounds and/or surfaces—they shake, cower, hide, try to run away, or will not try or approach something new—then it is time to intervene and start doing some serious confidence building. Your puppy's fears are not going to fix themselves.

Start with surfaces. Building your pup's confidence on new surfaces has a trickle effect to other areas of confidence building. Surfaces involve movement, whereas sights and sounds usually do not. When your pup is conquering a new surface, they are physically dominating that surface, which is a huge confidence booster.

Go to Chapter 9 (Socialization and Exposure) and focus on Phase 1 Surfaces and Phase 2 Surfaces. Start small and work your way up to harder and more challenging surfaces. If the surface is too easy for your pup and they are doing it with ease, you are giving them more practice but not necessarily boosting their confidence. Look for something harder and more challenging. Stick to one new surface per training session and do not end the session until your pup is confidently tackling that new surface and walking over it with ease. Use lots of food to reward your dog for good behavior. If your pup refuses to approach the new surface, apply some slip lead pressure (continuous light pressure) until your pup takes a step towards the new surface. Release the pressure and repeat.

Once your pup has tackled more surfaces and has spent a good amount of time gaining confidence that way, identify which sights and sounds they have an issue with. Start small, with something that is not overly intimidating, and work your way up to something bigger, harder, or louder, or whatever applies to that area of fear.

Your goal is to systematically help your dog learn how to work through their fears. Quitting is not an option. Once you tackle something, finish it. Be mindful about presenting challenges that are doable. Do not overwhelm your dog or overload their senses. Once their fight-or-flight instincts kick in, it is too late and you might have to stop and try again later.

Do your best. When in doubt, seek professional, in-person guidance from an experienced, balanced dog trainer.

21. OVERALL CONFIDENCE BUILDING

All dogs can benefit from confidence building—even confident dogs. You can never do too much of it. I do confidence building work with every puppy I train, but I especially focus on it if the puppy lacks confidence or tends to be a more nervous dog genetically.

When I am building a dog's confidence, I like to start by ensuring the dog has a strong obedience training foundation first and can easily do behaviors like taking food correctly, luring, and moving into different positions following the food.

From there, the first area of confidence building that I like to address first is new surfaces. I have found that keeping a dog's body in motion is the most effective way to keep their mind engaged and focused on the task at hand as opposed to becoming overwhelmed or locked up.

I pick small challenges first. The K9FITbone, for example, is a great obstacle. I bring my dog up to the obstacle and use a combination of leash pressure, praise, and food reward to coax the dog over the obstacle. My goal is to get them to put a foot on it or stand with both feet on it, then step off it. They are not allowed to hop over the bone or bypass it. They must step *on it.* When dogs physically dominate something by standing over it, it builds their confidence. This is much the same as a pack leader standing over a lesser-ranked pack member. They are asserting their dominance. That same mindset can help build your puppy's confidence.

You need to take a slow but steady approach. Start with surfaces then move on to new challenges. Whatever your puppy is unsure of and seeing for the first time, address it one at a time. The goal is to do lots of confidence-building sessions throughout the day and end on a good note.

Nervous dogs who lack a lot of confidence can be a challenge to work with. Patience is key! You want to start by identifying their fears and working through them systematically, one step at a time, breaking down the problem into small components and addressing them individually. Like building blocks, each small success builds on the last.

For specific help with fear issues, such as fear of dogs, fear of people, and/or fear of new sights, sounds, and surfaces, see problems #18, 19, and 20 respectively.

22. PEEING AND POOPING IN THE HOUSE OR CRATE

Is your puppy peeing and/or pooping in the house or crate? Yuck! Sounds like something has gone awry with potty training (Chapter 5) or crate training (Chapter 6). Start there and try to troubleshoot. What are you doing differently or incorrectly compared to the advice and recommendations I have given you?

Most of the time when a pup is having accidents in the house, it is because they have been given too much freedom too soon and are not getting enough potty breaks outside. They need to be kept on a leash in the house and taken out more frequently.

Accidents in the crate could be due to not getting enough potty breaks, incorrectly timed potty breaks, or coprophagia (see problem #4).

Remember, it is of utmost importance that you establish a fine-tuned potty-training and crate-training schedule that works for *both* you and your puppy, and that you feed only within a certain window of time during the day and limit access to water. This allows you to predict when your puppy is going to need to go potty so that you can offer a potty break at just the right time.

23. REACTIVITY

If your puppy *reacts* when seeing another dog in public—and the reaction is more intense than you would expect—they are demonstrating what we call "*reactivity.*" The most common signs of reactivity are whining, barking, lunging, and pulling on the leash. Dog reactivity for puppies usually stems from excitement. They have had lots of playdates with other dogs and when they see a dog in public, *they want to play!*

When a puppy is excited-reactive towards other dogs, I am not overly concerned about it. Dogs are simple association creatures. For a well-socialized puppy, it is normal for them to react in some way when they see another dog in public. While it can be frustrating to lose your puppy's focus when this happens, do not fret. It is a good indicator that your puppy is indeed *social.* I will take a social puppy over a fearful puppy any day.

In the next chapter, I teach you how to use a "Do Not Pet" vest in public to work on neutrality with your puppy (teaching them to ignore other people and dogs). If your puppy is over four months of age and well socialized, try this approach. You will see significant changes in just a few weeks.

The other end of the spectrum of reactivity is called "fear reactivity." If your puppy sees or is approached by another dog and reacts by growling, snapping, lunging, or hiding behind you with their hackles up, they are fear-reactive. This can be more challenging to work through because the reactivity is coming from a place of fear and insecurity due to a lack of socialization, improper socialization, bad experiences with other dogs, and/or poor genetics.

I would recommend doubling down on socialization and confidence building before it is too late. Once the critical socialization window closes—at or around sixteen weeks of age—you have missed the best opportunities to socialize your puppy. You can still play catch-up, but the clock is running out and you may never have a *super social puppy.* Older puppies typically have a much harder time socializing than younger puppies do.

If your puppy is afraid of other dogs, see problem #18 (fear of dogs) for additional help.

24. RESOURCE GUARDING

If your puppy becomes stiff, whale-eyes you (when the whites of their eyes, called the "sclera," become visible), growls at you, or snaps at you when approaching or trying to take something from them, such as food, bones, toys, or other resources, they are resource guarding. Also called "possession aggression" or "food aggression," *resource guarding* is when a dog reacts to a perceived threat while they have a valued resource in their possession. They feel they are about to lose something and take action to keep it.

Here is what I want you to understand: resource guarding is a natural and instinctive behavior. In the wild, wolves have to protect what is theirs: their territory and their food. If they do not, they could die.

When a dog resource guards, they are showing a natural instinct to protect what is theirs. I actually *like* seeing a small amount of resource guarding in puppies that I pick for personal protection. When a puppy says "No" to a stranger taking their bone or food, that tells me the dog will have no problem protecting their home and family when they grow up.

When a puppy shows signs of resource guarding that is directed at me, I put a stop to it immediately and put them in their place. They learn very quickly that I am the alpha and they need to be respectful of me and everyone around me. The same thought process goes for dogs within my pack. They are allowed to *communicate* with each other and do not have to share their meals, but they are not allowed to *fight* over resources. There is a difference.

Everything in this program—from hand-feeding to introducing raw—teaches you how to set your puppy up to win. They learn that you are the leader and the provider of good things. You are not a threat and your relationship is one based on trust and respect, not aggression or dominance.

If your puppy is struggling with resource guarding or if your puppy has an unusually strong guarding instinct, my best advice is to work in person with a trainer. Your dog needs clear communication and straightforward guidance. Left unchecked, resource guarding can quickly spiral out of control and become dangerous.

25. SEPARATION ANXIETY

If your dog pants, drools, whines, barks, cries, or tries to escape from the crate or place bed any time you or someone else goes out of their sight or they are left alone, they have separation anxiety. Separation anxiety is best described as FOMO (fear of missing out). It is common in dogs with high pack drive. They want to be with their people and do not like being left alone.

It is not cute and needs to be addressed immediately. As time goes on, without training, the anxiety will get worse—not better!

Separation anxiety can be simple or complex. The complex cases usually involve a genetic component. Yes, separation anxiety can be a genetic behavior that is passed down from generation to generation, just like aggression, fear, and resource guarding.

In some cases of separation anxiety, strict crate-training protocol must be followed. You have to adequately meet your dog's needs for physical exercise, mental stimulation, and training prior to putting them in the crate, and you absolutely *cannot* let them out of the crate until they are calm. If you worry that they are digging, chewing, or trying to break out of the crate, you might use a properly fitted Baskerville muzzle to stop them from hurting themselves or escaping the crate. In most cases, an escape-proof crate is required for this training.

You can also put a muzzle on if they bark when you step out of sight and they are on the place bed. In this case, I recommend a nylon muzzle that holds their mouth shut so that they cannot bark. Supervise them from a safe distance so they do not choke on their own spit or vomit. Once they learn that they cannot bark, they will settle down. Of course, they will try to get the muzzle off, but as long as it is tight enough, they will be unsuccessful and give up. They need to feel that their efforts are in vain and that you are not interested in their pity party.

Once that happens and they lay down or stop barking, you can re-enter the room and tell them "Good dog" without making eye contact. (This reinforcement might reactivate their FOMO, but I feel it is important to give feedback to dogs who are struggling to figure out the solution to a problem: how to get the muzzle off and why they are wearing it in the first place.) A simple "Good dog" will help them understand that their behavior in the moment is good, acceptable, and pleasing to you. It is necessary.

Over time, they will learn to be quiet on place because they will want to avoid being muzzled and because you are teaching them a new association with the place bed, one of calmness and not fear or anxiety. The same goes for the crate. Over time, you will be able to take off the muzzle, and your dog will learn to settle in the crate.

It is important for all dogs—but especially dogs with separation anxiety—that you do not make a big deal of your comings and goings. It is unfair to the dog. Make a calm, quiet exit and, when you come back, ignore your dog for several minutes until they calm down before you give them any attention whatsoever.

German shepherds are notorious for having separation anxiety, yet not a single German shepherd that I have raised has ever had it. Why? Because I only reinforce behavior that I like, I stop bad behavior immediately, and I present myself as a calm, assertive leader to my dogs.

If your dog has separation anxiety, it is not something to be proud of. It does not mean your dog loves you. It means your dog is unstable, unbalanced, and unable to be in a calm state of mind on their own.

They are uncomfortable in their own skin. Dogs with separation anxiety are usually insecure. Address your puppy's separation anxiety right away before it becomes a serious problem.

Chapter Summary

Problem-solving is a matter of identifying the problem, understanding the root cause, and coming up with a working solution. In some cases, the solution is multi-pronged and requires increased efforts in many areas for maximum effectiveness.

Puppies are a product of their environments and can only rise to the level of their training.

Do your best. When in doubt, seek professional help to troubleshoot. Catching things when they happen—and not later, after the problems grow and multiply—makes problem-solving easier and more successful.

15.

THE MORE YOU KNOW!

"It's the extra effort after you have done your best that creates victory."

—Lou Holtz

This chapter is for all of you overachievers who want to do more with your dog!

When they are under six months of age, your puppy is too young to begin intensive obedience training, but they are smart, eager, and ready to learn more. In this chapter, I give you doable, age-appropriate challenges to advance your puppy's training while you wait to begin more advanced training.

Read through this entire chapter, then work on one item at a time with your dog.

BEFORE WE BEGIN...

Before we begin, let's make sure we are on the same page. The topics below assume that your puppy is confident, social, and has excelled in all of the puppy training you did before this.

If you have any doubts about your puppy's abilities or if you have taken a break from training and your puppy is a bit rusty, go back to Chapters 8 (Obedience Training) and 9 (Socialization and Exposure). Go through the material and bring your puppy up to speed. It should not take too long and it is worthwhile.

Once you feel ready, go ahead and jump into this chapter!

GENERALIZATION

The first topic up for consideration is called "generalization." *Generalization* is your dog's ability to exhibit training behaviors in any location and with different handlers. It is the ability to reproduce desired behaviors in different environments, settings, and conditions from those they were originally trained in.

Dogs do not generalize on their own. We have to help them! Your field trips have helped tremendously with teaching your pup the concept of generalization and perhaps they have done really well with it, but maybe there is room for improvement.

Ask yourself, "Where have I trained my puppy the most? In which location(s) are they most comfortable?"

Also ask yourself, "With whom has my puppy trained the most? How many handlers have they had?"

The first step to generalizing training involves changing your primary training "classroom." You need to start training in other rooms of your house. Minimize distractions in those rooms, then add distractions back in. Your puppy should be able to generalize quickly without many hiccups along the way.

From there, take your training outside and make sure you are practicing in the backyard, in the front yard, in the driveway, and down the road. Obedience is obedience. A command is a command. It should not matter where you are when you are giving that command.

Have the slip lead on your puppy, of course, and use a food reward. Work through basic commands (luring, Name Game, sit-stay, down-stay, Preheeling, Recall Drills, and so on).

Go to one new location per training session and end the session on a good note.

From there, try introducing new handlers. Are there family members who have not worked with your pup yet? Perhaps Grandma and Grandpa want to give it a go? Are your neighbors open to working with your puppy a little? If you have willing volunteers, take advantage of it!

This doubles as an excellent opportunity for you to coach someone new. Teach them how to hold and deliver food. Show them how to hold the slip lead. Help them do luring, Name Game, and two-treat recall. Avoid more complicated behaviors like Preheeling and place bed training. Do this training at home. In public, you want your puppy's focus to be on *you* and no one else.

PROPRIOCEPTION

Once you have generalized your puppy's training to different locations and new handlers, it is time to start working on a new version of generalization: proprioception ("proh-pree-uh-sep-shuhn"). *Proprioception* aims at improving a dog's body awareness, balance, and coordination. In training, proprioception helps dogs obey commands from different positions relative to you: like telling your dog to "Sit" when they are next to you instead of in front of you, or asking your dog to "Down" on a picnic table instead of in your training room, or teaching them Preheeling on the opposite side.

It takes practice and repetition to sharpen your dog's proprioception skills. Be patient. Start small and work up to harder commands, behaviors, and positions. Lure your dog if you need to help them out or apply a little slip lead pressure.

Once they catch on, you will see a rapid progression of learning.

Always end your sessions on a good note.

Have fun and be creative!

I put my dogs in all sorts of crazy situations to challenge their proprioception and understanding of commands. For example, my dogs know a "Back" command (to back up), so I put them in front of stairs and ask them to "Back." They must figure out how to go *up* the stairs *backwards* moving one leg at a time. It is fun and challenging!

UNINTENTIONAL EXTINCTION

We talked about intentional extinction in Chapter 14 (Problems and Solutions). Another way that extinction can happen is called unintentional extinction. *Unintentional extinction* is where you accidentally cause your dog to stop doing a desired behavior, like coming when called, because, over time, you have stopped reinforcing it. If you stop rewarding your dog for coming when called, they are eventually going to stop coming when called.

To this day, I still praise and pet my dogs for coming when called. I want them to know that their obedience to my commands is desirable and rewarded. Every time I give my dogs a command, I mark it at the very least with "Good" so they know I am pleased with their behavior.

Do not forget to mark, praise, reward, and otherwise reinforce your dog's training. All obedience, even basic commands, need to be acknowledged in some way, shape, or form.

JACKPOTTING

I have mentioned jackpotting before, but I want to highlight it here because it comes into play when you are adding more skills to your dog's resume and giving them new challenges. *Jackpotting* is reserved for breakthrough moments in training when your dog offers the exact behavior you are asking for.

Let's say you are working on "Speak" and your dog barks. Jackpot!

Jackpotting involves giving your dog an abundance of food, praise, and affection—throwing a celebratory party, essentially—to strongly reinforce the behavior they just performed.

The key to jackpotting is to end the session after the jackpot. End on a good note! Do not try to get that same behavior a second time. Your dog will end up feeling defeated. The dopamine rush from a jackpot cannot be beat!

POST-TRAINING

What is the best thing you can do with your dog after a training session, you ask? Pay attention because this is fascinating!

After a mentally stimulating training session where the dog was thinking but not stressed, put them in their crate. This allows them to decompress, replay the session in their head, and learn from it again.

After a somewhat stressful training session, play is your best option. Play tug, fetch, or flirt pole with your dog. This releases dopamine, which counteracts stress and helps your dog return to a normal mental state.

MODELING BEHAVIOR

One of the ways dogs learn is by modeling behavior. When you are training more than one dog, allow your dogs to watch each other train or face their crate out into your training area.

Dogs can watch other dogs in the learning process and learn something by watching them! This increases the overall learning curve, especially when everyone is working on the same behavior, skill, or command.

Be mindful that your dogs are always setting a good example for each other during these sessions.

FADING OUT FOOD

By the time your puppy has reached four months of age, most of their training has involved food and praise. Do not be in a hurry to fade out food too quickly. In the grand scheme of things, you have only done two months of food-based training so far. Two months! We want our dog's obedience to stick for life. Two months is nothing!

By the same token, you should not be a PEZ dispenser for your dog. Let me give you some practical tips on how you can *begin* fading out food for your dog's training sessions.

First, take off your treat pouch. Put your dog's kibble in your pockets instead. This way your dog does not look for a treat pouch (antecedent) before offering a behavior. *You* are the source of all good things, not the treat pouch.

Next, reward more selectively. Reward A+ behavior only! If your dog sits on command but does so slowly, mark "Good" but do not reward. When they sit quickly, mark "Good" and reward. There is a difference between quick, sharp, *pretty* obedience and flat, boring, lazy obedience. Reward what you love, not what you like.

As a general rule, you can lower your ROR (rate of reinforcement) during training. Reward strong, constant eye contact. Reward your dog for making good decisions (like staying in a sit-stay instead of getting up when the cat walks into the room). Reward engagement and nice obedience. Reward your dog, but do not reward *everything.* A+ behavior only!

Let me give you an example.

Let's say I am working on recall with my puppy. She is off leash in the backyard. I give the "Come" command and she looks up at me, looks at another dog, and then casually saunters over to me. I will say "Good girl" and pet her, but I will not give her food. Did she obey? Yes. Did she obey immediately, enthusiastically, and quickly? Nope.

If I tell her to "Come" and she immediately stops what she is doing and sprints towards me, I will praise and reward her generously. I might even jackpot her!

Do not eliminate food completely from training; it is too soon for that. Just be more selective about when you reward your dog (and when you do not). You will be pleasantly surprised by the outcome.

WEARING A "DO NOT PET" VEST

I am really, really excited to write about this because it is such an incredibly useful concept, and one that you will really benefit from! If you have a social, confident, happy, obedient puppy, this tip is for you. You have done a great job up to this point by taking your puppy through the first two months of life and training and creating an exuberant dog who loves everyone and everything. Their *joie de vivre* is obvious, and you might be catching yourself saying things like, "She just wants to say hi!" as you try to control your now large puppy who is choking herself out on the leash. Sound familiar?

If it does, then it is time for some neutrality training, and the "Do Not Pet" vest is your ticket to success.

You can purchase a red (or black) vest with a basic "DO NOT PET" patch. Put the patch on whichever side faces *away* from you and *towards* other people. Do not overload the vest with other patches; one "DO NOT PET" patch is all you need. Less is more.

Start putting that vest on your puppy every time you take them on field trips. The vest means that your dog is in training and that people should not pet them and dogs should not say hi to them. It means that you are training, not socializing. After a few field trips, your dog will begin to understand that the vest means, "Nobody's going to pet me and no dogs are going to say hi to me," which will help your dog calm down and focus on you. When the field trip is over, take the vest off.

Initially, the vest will have zero effect on your dog's behavior because it has not been conditioned yet. Over time—with practice and consistency—your dog will learn to ignore people and dogs because people and dogs are ignoring them!

Avoid making eye contact with people, focus on your dog, and people will leave you alone.

After four or five field trips—maybe more for super social dogs—your dog will begin to associate the vest with neutrality. That is your golden ticket! You will see them relax and even ignore people who are trying to give them attention!

Once you have accomplished this level of neutrality, you might occasionally do a socialization field trip where you leave the vest at home and take your dog out in public, let people pet them, and allow them to be their social, bubbly, happy self. That said, it is best to not let your dog greet other dogs in public whether you know them or not. Socialization is best saved for supervised playdates.

This ensures that your dog continues to have positive socialization experiences while they are in the socialization window, which lasts until twelve months of age. Soon your dog will learn that when the vest is on, it is time to work, and when the vest is off, it is okay to play—just like a service dog!

TRAINING COLLARS

Training collars have no place on a puppy. If your puppy is under six months of age, resist the urge to buy a "quick fix" prong collar or e-collar. Your puppy is much too young to be properly trained on a correction collar. They are learning obedience, confidence building, and socialization. When you put a training collar on a young puppy and start correcting them, they can have superstitious associations, become fearful, or shut down.

No training is better than bad training. Putting a training collar on a young puppy is a bad idea. We add training collars after six months of age in the Good Dog program. Wait until then! When used correctly, training collars are wonderful for proofing and generalizing training to make it reliable without food.

Chapter Summary

The more you know! I hope you enjoyed this chapter. I sure enjoyed writing it! The world of dog training is fascinating. There is so much to learn and so much you can do with your dog. I hope this information serves as a starting-off point for you to deep-dive into more training with your dog.

CONCLUSION

"This is not the end, this is not even the beginning of the end, this is just perhaps the end of the beginning."
—Winston S. Churchill

So, what's next? If you are ready to keep growing, there are countless ways to continue your journey as a handler—and possibly even as a dog trainer. I am here to offer you a variety of opportunities to build on what you have learned and take your training to the next level.

Let's take a look!

Valor K9 Academy Online®

You already know about the Puppy Head Start program and the VK9 First Aid and CPR course—but did you know we offer a variety of other training courses and private coaching options?

The Good Dog™ Program is designed for social dogs six months and older. It focuses on owner education, foundational obedience, prong collar training for on-leash reliability, e-collar training for off-leash freedom, manners at home and in public, and more. It is the cherry on top of all of the great work you have already done. Everything comes together into a final product that is both beautiful and unique—just like your dog. Best of all, your dog will be *reliably* obedient without the need for food rewards.

As a service dog handler myself, service dogs are especially close to my heart. My own service dog helped me reclaim my independence after military trauma left me broken. That is why I created the Service Dog Select™ program, designed to empower everyday people to train their own service dogs. This comprehensive course includes owner education, advanced obedience, task training for physical and mental disabilities, and public access readiness.

And this is just the beginning—we are working on more courses to be released in the near future!

If you are looking for one-on-one support, do not miss our virtual private coaching service. You will get dedicated attention and expert guidance to troubleshoot challenges, refine your training, and continue making real progress—no matter where you are in your journey. My team and I are here to help you.

Valor K9 Academy

At Valor K9 Academy, we offer a wide range of in-person training services from our Boise, Idaho location. These include private lessons, small group classes, Stay & Play boarding, and immersive Board & Train programs. In addition, I offer specialized workshops, seminars, and shadow programs for dog trainers and dedicated dog owners who want to take their skills to the next level.

To stay up-to-date on upcoming events and opportunities, be sure to subscribe to our newsletter at www.valork9academyonline.com. I would love to see you at an event soon!

Books

I plan to write a book to accompany each course offered through Valor K9 Academy Online. My goal is to provide you with practical, in-depth resources you can turn to again and again as you train and grow with your dog. Stay tuned—more is coming soon!

Thank You

Thank you for allowing me to be part of your puppy training journey. From the moment you picked up your puppy to the everyday work of raising and training them, it is truly an honor to walk alongside you. I hope this book has given you the tools, clarity, and confidence you need—and that you have felt supported and encouraged every step of the way.

Puppy training has been a lifelong passion of mine. It is more than just a career—it is a calling. My deepest hope in writing this book was to share what I have learned through years of hands-on experience to help make your path a little smoother, your bond with your dog a little deeper, and your confidence a little stronger. If this book has done even a small part of that, I am truly grateful.

If there is ever anything more I can do to support you and your pup, please do not hesitate to reach out. You can connect with me anytime through the contact page on our website at https://www.valork9academyonline.com/contact.

Enjoy your new puppy. God bless, and happy training!

ACKNOWLEDGMENTS

To my parents, for setting the example, raising me right, and always believing in me.

To my husband, for encouraging me every step of the way and for knowing that someday this book would be a reality.

To Linda, for being my friend and sounding board. Your encouragement when this book was just an idea means the world to me.

To my clients, for always trusting me with your dogs. I have the best clients in the world. Thank you for allowing me to do what I love.

To my Instagram followers, for your love and support. Thank you for letting me share my love for dogs and for letting me step away from socials when I need to.

To all the dogs, for the challenges, hardships, rewards, and lessons learned. Experience is the best teacher. I would not be the trainer I am today without every single one of you.

To Vernon, Jed, Mike, and Anthony, who opened up the world of publishing to me and gave me the opportunity to publish a book. It is a dream come true!

To my daughter Emma, who is already a better dog trainer than I was at her age. Shoot for the moon, baby girl. You are strong, smart, and beautiful. The world is yours and there is nothing you cannot do!

And finally, to God, who gives me strength. Thank you for your mercy and grace and for giving me my love for dogs.

ABOUT THE AUTHOR

Author Photo Credit:
Rase Littlefield Photography

Amy Pishner is the founder, owner, and head trainer of Valor K9 Academy and Valor Protection Dogs. After becoming a triple-certified dog trainer in 2013, Amy has spent her career training thousands of dogs of all ages, needs, and temperaments whether they are family, police, service, or personal protection dogs. She holds bachelor's degrees in international political economy and Spanish from Carthage College in Wisconsin and served in the United States Air Force and Wisconsin Air National Guard. Amy currently resides in Idaho with her husband and daughter.